SKITS

THAT TEACH

Children

Colleen Ison

Skits That Teach Children is a revision
of *Goliath's Last Stand*

**STANDARD
PUBLISHING**
Cincinnati, Ohio

The Standard Publishing Company, Cincinnati, Ohio
A division of Standex International Corporation
Revised © 1993 by The Standard Publishing Company
All rights reserved
Printed in the United States of America

00 99 98 97 96 95   5 4 3

Library of Congress Cataloging-in-Publication Data

Ison, Colleen, 1962-
    Skits that teach children : including "Goliath's last stand" and fifteen other short dramas / by Colleen Ison.
    p. cm.
    Summary: Includes sixteen short plays on such religious themes as prayer, forgiveness, and the omnipresence of God. Discussion questions follow each play.
    ISBN 0-87403-947-9
    1. Drama in Christian education. 2. Children's plays, American. 3. Christian drama, American. [1. Christian life--Drama. 2. Plays.] I. Title.
BV1534.4.I864   1993
268'.432--dc20
                                            93-20097
                                            CIP

Foreword

Involving children (of *any* age!) in the lesson is one of the absolute best ways to teach. While they are learning Bible facts and principles, they are also having fun, accepting responsibility, expressing themselves creatively, and planting the Word of God deep within their hearts.

The sixteen short plays in this book will provide these experiences for your students. Some plays are suitable for impromptu classroom performances (either read aloud by the students, or performed by guests), while others are more theatrical and should be prepared for special programs.

The wide range of length and simplicity, and the variety of subject matter (less than half are Bible-time plays), should allow you to find the right play for almost any occasion and any age. Children as young as three and four can take part in some of these plays. With just as much coaching as it takes to teach a new song, children can memorize the short lines they are to say in unison on cue from an adult or teen narrator. To make things even easier for these little ones, use their own names instead of the names given to the characters. This may also help them to realize that the situations and Biblical principles apply to them.

If you have any teaching experience at all, you have already realized that preparing a play for a special performance is going to require extra time. Since you won't want to use all of your class time for this, and one rehearsal a week would take far too long (and your students would lose interest), you'll probably need to schedule extra rehearsals. Children memorize easily, however, especially when they're excited about having a part, and you'll find that your extra effort will be well worthwhile. The audience will tell you so as the farmer's servant rolls a "good seed" into place, and "it" begins to grow, unrolling and stretching into a smiling stalk of wheat!

Happy acting!

Contents

Goliath's Last Stand

This lighthearted version of the David and Goliath story aims to teach the children that God gives us the power to do whatever we have to do, no matter what the circumstances. An adult narrator should memorize his or her lines so they can be said with as much animation as possible. Children provide the backdrop to the story, playing the parts of David, and the Israelite and Philistine armies. These children can be any age as long as they are able to recite a few lines in unison on cue from the narrator. Signs for the audience to read aloud are also part of the script. They enable those watching to participate. An adult should hold the signs up at the right times and lead the audience in reading them out loud. Explain this to the audience before the play and practice reading a few. The narrator needs to keep this play moving along quickly.

Characters

NARRATOR—An adult who can tell a story with energy and enthusiasm and memorize many lines.

GOLIATH—A man or teenage boy, as big as possible.

DAVID—A boy who can say a few lines convincingly and mime slaying Goliath. If he can memorize his lines, the narrator won't have to cue him.

SIGN PERSON—Someone to hold up the signs and lead the audience in reading them.

ISRAELITES—Any number of children.

PHILISTINES—Same number as the Israelites, but they may all be taller and bigger.

Costumes

Goliath needs armor covering torso and legs, a helmet and

perhaps a shield. Otherwise costumes aren't really necessary. If desired, short tunics with belts and sandals could be worn, with different colors or accessories to distinguish the armies.

Props
A slingshot (don't worry about the rock, just pretend).
A huge spear for Goliath.
A full grocery bag.
Ten signs, reading: Israelites, Philistines, Hooray!, Boo!, How could this be?, We are talking big., Uh-oh!, Who does he think he is?, He hasn't got a chance., He did it!

(The cast is out among the audience as narrator begins the play. The narrator won't stay in a fixed position but will move around the stage, being careful not to block the action.)

NARRATOR: Ladies and Gentlemen, today I'm going to tell you a story from the Bible about two men. One of them was a man who served God, and his name was David. David loved, obeyed, and trusted God. The other man did not serve God. He didn't love or obey God, and the only thing he trusted in was his own strength. (You'll know the one I'm talking about when I get to him.) What I want you to learn from the story is that if you serve God, you never need to be afraid of anyone who is against you, even if it seems like they are stronger. As I tell the story, my helper here *(points to sign-holder)* is going to help with the telling of the story. Ready? Then here we go.

Once there were two armies that were fighting against each other. One was an army of God's people. They were called the Israelites. Who were the people in God's army?

AUDIENCE SIGN: Israelites

NARRATOR: Right. The other was an army of people who did not serve God. They didn't even believe in Him. They wanted to capture the Israelites and take their land. They were called Philistines. Who were the people in the army against God's people?

8

AUDIENCE SIGN: Philistines

NARRATOR: Right. Now the Israelites were gathered on one hill . . . *(Israelites come out of the audience and quickly gather on stage right.)*

AUDIENCE SIGN: Hooray!

NARRATOR: . . . And the Philistines were gathered on another hill. . . . *(Philistines quickly gather on stage left.)*

AUDIENCE SIGN: Boo!

NARRATOR: . . . And there was a valley in between them. It's a very sad thing to have to say, but the army of God's people were not doing too well. They kept saying they were dismayed and terrified.

ISRAELITES *(in unison):* We are dismayed and terrified.

NARRATOR: But the Philistines were feeling pretty happy with themselves. They thought they were the greatest.

PHILISTINES *(in unison):* We are the greatest!

AUDIENCE SIGN: How could this be?

NARRATOR: How this could be is a very good question. And there is a very good answer—which you will understand when you meet Goliath. *(A great roar is heard off stage left. The Israelites look fearful. The Philistines smile.)*

PHILISTINES *(in unison):* That's Goliath.

NARRATOR: Yes, that is Goliath. Listen to what the Bible says about Goliath: He was over nine feet tall. He was so big that the armor he wore to protect himself weighed 125 pounds. *(Goliath roars again off stage.)* He wore thick metal covers on his legs, and his spear—get this—you know how the heads of spears are kind of little? Well, Goliath's spear head weighed fifteen pounds. In short, Ladies and Gentlemen, Goliath was a big guy. What are we talking here?

AUDIENCE SIGN: We are talking big.

NARRATOR: Right. Goliath was the kind of person who would send (name a current macho hero) running for cover.

(Goliath roars again and enters to stand with the Philistines, who pat him on the back, etc. The Israelites look terrified.)

NARRATOR: But the worst thing about Goliath wasn't what he looked like, but what he said.

GOLIATH *(calling as if they were at a distance):* Hey, Israelites, you pack of chicken-hearted scum, let's settle this fight once and for all! I dare you to choose one of your men to meet me in the valley for a fight to the death. Whoever wins, his people get to rule over the loser's side. Let's see if your God helps you now!

AUDIENCE SIGN: Uh-oh!

NARRATOR: Things didn't look too good for the Israelites. Goliath was very strong and very evil. The Israelites were just petrified.

ISRAELITES *(in unison):* We're just petrified!

NARRATOR: They didn't have a fighter nearly as big and strong as Goliath. The Philistines told them they were sunk.

PHILISTINES *(to Israelites):* You're sunk!

NARRATOR: While the Israelites get into a huddle and try to decide what to do, and the Philistines get into a huddle and play Trivial Pursuit . . .

(Both armies get into huddles and keep still.)

NARRATOR: . . . I'll tell you about David, the hero of our story. David was an Israelite, but he was too young to fight in the army. He stayed home and took care of his father's sheep while his brothers went off to fight. Now David was a very special young man. He knew that God was always with him, and this made him very brave. Sometimes when he was guarding his sheep, a bear or a lion would come, and David would kill it with whatever weapon he had—including his bare hands! One day, David's father sent him to where the Israelites were fighting to take his brothers some food.

(David enters right with a grocery bag and stands near the entrance.)

NARRATOR: It just so happened that while David was there, Goliath spoke again.

GOLIATH: Hey Israelites, you bunch of babies, which one of you is going to fight me and get creamed into the ground?

(Huddles break up—Israelites scream and cower, Philistines laugh.)

GOLIATH *(laughs):* Look at God's chosen people, running away!

(David watches the scene, astonished. He puts down his bag and moves a few steps forward.)

NARRATOR: David couldn't believe what he was hearing. He said, "How dare this man insult God like that!"

DAVID: How dare this man insult God like that!

AUDIENCE SIGN: Who does he think he is?

NARRATOR: Goliath thought he was the strongest man in the world. He probably was, but he hadn't counted on what was going to happen next. David stepped forward and said he would fight Goliath.

DAVID: I'll fight Goliath. *(Both armies turn to look at David.)*

NARRATOR: The Philistines looked at David. He was so small compared to Goliath, they just laughed. *(Philistines laugh.)*

NARRATOR: The Israelites told David he was only a boy—he couldn't fight a giant.

ISRAELITES *(in unison):* You can't fight a giant!

NARRATOR: But David was not afraid. He knew the Lord wanted the Israelites to win this war. He said, "The Lord who saved me from the lions and the bears will save me from this Philistine."

DAVID: The Lord who saved me from the lions and the bears will save me from this Philistine.

NARRATOR: So David and Goliath went down into the valley, and met each other face to face. Goliath yelled at David in his fearful voice.

GOLIATH: I despise you David! I'm going to murder you and feed you to the animals.

NARRATOR: But David told Goliath that he wasn't just fighting an Israelite, he was fighting God, and God would prove to the whole world that He could defeat anyone. He said, "God is going to defeat you, Goliath."

DAVID: God is going to defeat you, Goliath.

(David and Goliath face off at center stage, and act out what is narrated.)

NARRATOR: They circled around each other . . . then they circled back the other way. David had his little slingshot—Goliath had his huge spear. It looked like David didn't have a chance.

AUDIENCE SIGN: He hasn't got a chance!

NARRATOR: But then, just as Goliath was drawing back with his huge spear with its fifteen-pound head, David took aim with his slingshot, fired a stone, hit Goliath right in the forehead—and the great giant keeled over!

(Goliath falls forward onto the ground. The Philistines and Israelites look at one another in surprise.)

AUDIENCE SIGN: He did it!

PHILISTINES: He did it!

ISRAELITES: He did it!

NARRATOR: Yes, he did it! Then the Philistines, who suddenly realized they had lost, turned around and took off over the hill.

AUDIENCE SIGN: Boo!

NARRATOR: The Israelites, who suddenly realized they had won, took off after the Philistines.

(Israelites run after the Philistines, cheering.)

AUDIENCE SIGN: Hooray!

(David approaches Goliath, puts a foot on his back and raises his arms in victory as Narrator finishes.)

NARRATOR: So David defeated Goliath, who was so much bigger and stronger, because the Lord helped him. And that is the end of this story.

Questions for Discussion

1. Who were the Israelites?

2. Who were the Philistines?

3. What were the Israelites afraid of?

4. How did Goliath want to settle the fight?

5. What was special about David? Was he stronger than Goliath?

6. What made David able to defeat Goliath?

7. What sort of things can we ask God to help us with?

Christmas Day
for Jessica May

This Christmas play, written in rhyme, is about a girl whose selfish attitude toward Christmas is changed when she hears the Christmas story. A chorus of two to four people recite the lines while the action takes place. This play can really be enhanced with lighting, including a spotlight. The play has two sets, a bedroom scene and a nativity scene, both of which have to be quickly set up and taken away during moments when part of the stage is in darkness and action is taking place elsewhere. The chorus may be any age group, but members have many lines to memorize and need to be very expressive and confident. Chorus lines may be divided among groups or individuals in the chorus, or said all together.

Jessica will need to practice timing her actions to match the rhyme. The play also has lesser parts for two adults or older children and more children's parts in the nativity scene.

Characters

JESSICA—a girl who can play both a spoiled brat and a sweetheart. Her facial and body movements need to be very expressive.

CHORUS—Two to four people who are good at memorizing and reciting rhyme. They should put as much of their personalities into their performance as possible. The chorus will be more interesting if you get people with contrasting looks and voices.

DAD

MOM

READER—A girl with a smooth, pretty speaking voice.

SHEPHERDS—Three to six children.

MARY

JOSEPH

Costumes

Jessica wears a pretty dress. For the scene in her bedroom, she removes her shoes and puts on a robe. Parents will do the same. Jessica and her parents will wear winter coats and hats on the way to and from the nativity play. The reader wears a long white dress. The shepherds, Mary, and Joseph are in Biblical costume. The chorus can decide its own costume—all red and green would be fun. They could even be dressed up as elves or something.

Props

A long, long piece of paper (one of those endless computer printouts would be ideal), a pencil, a Bible, and three chairs downstage right from which Jessica and her parents will view the play.

The nativity scene requires a three-sided structure suggesting the stable walls, a manger and hay on the ground, and a doll inside the manger.

The bedroom scene requires a bed made up, a chair and a desk with paper and crayons on it.

Chorus enters and assembles down left.

CHORUS: Children come gather, and listen today,
To the story of Jessica—Jessica May.
A girl who thought Christmas was simply the
best,
And made sure her presents would top all the
rest.

(Jessica enters left, writing on a huge list that trails behind her all the way across the stage. She stops near the other side of the stage and remains preoccupied with making the list.)

CHORUS: To Jessica, presents were all Christmas meant,
And on Jessica's presents much money was
spent.
She'd make lists for her parents, quite long and
detailed.

And if they didn't get them, she'd tell them they
    failed.

Yes, she'd throw screaming fits in the middle of
    stores.
Kick chairs and bang pots and throw food and
    slam doors.
She knew what she wanted—she wanted a lot,
And what Jessica wanted, dear Jessica got.

*(On the last line of above stanza, Jessica looks up from her
list and smiles smugly. Then she consults her list as she says
the next lines:)*

JESSICA: Two dolls and three kittens, a large rocking horse,
          A playhouse with lights, and a *real* stove, of
             course.
          A pony, a TV, a red shining sleigh . . .

CHORUS: . . . Were just the beginning for Jessica May.

(Jessica exits right, her list trailing behind).

CHORUS: She was spoiled, it's true—it was really quite sad,
          For whatever she needed, she already had.
          And all of these presents were just shutting out,
          What Christmas is really and truly about.

          But thankfully, this little story is not,
          About just what our friend didn't need but still got.
          No, it gets a lot better we're thankful to say.
          For a new understanding struck Jessica May.

          It's strange how this happens, it can't be explained,
          How your whole way of thinking is suddenly
             changed.
          It started by seeing a Sunday school play,
          Revealing what happened that first Christmas Day.

          Jessica's parents had bundled her tight,
          To take her to church on a Christmas Eve night:

They'd wrapped presents, hung stockings, and
    made ginger snaps,
Now they walked through the snow in their mittens
    and caps.

(Jessica and her parents enter left in winter coats and walk down right. Jessica talks as they take off their coats and settle to watch the play.)

JESSICA: This better be interesting . . .

CHORUS: . . . Jessica said,

JESSICA: 'Cause I'd rather be home in my warm little bed.

CHORUS: But all thoughts of this nature were quickly wiped
        out.
        As Jessica watched what this play was about.

(Lights dim on last line of previous stanza. Chorus sings first verse of "The First Noel" as a spotlight comes up on the reader, who is holding an open Bible. Chorus quietly exits.)

READER: Long, long ago, on a night when the stars were very
    bright and the air was clear and still, shepherds were
    watching their flocks in the fields near Bethlehem.

(Spot fades off the reader and comes up on shepherds, sitting in a semi-circle, stage right. Ideally, the light should slant down from above left, so the audience can see the shaft, as though an angel above were the source of light.)

READER: The shepherds stayed close around a fire that gave a
    circle of light in the deep darkness, and somehow, the quiet
    of the night hushed their voices. *(Reads.)* "Then an angel of
    the Lord appeared to them, and the glory of the Lord shone
    around them and they were terrified."

(Shepherds look up the shaft of light and are overcome with awe. Meanwhile, the nativity scene is being set stage left.)

READER: "But the angel said to them: 'Do not worry. I bring you
    good news of great joy that will be for all people. Today in

the town of David a Savior has been born; he is Christ the Lord. This will be a sign to you; you will find the baby wrapped in cloths lying in a manger.'"

(Dim lights come up to reveal the nativity scene. Shepherds talk quietly among themselves as Reader continues. Mary and Joseph are only part of the picture of the scene. They can move, but should not be distracting. Have them sitting on the ground looking over the manger, Mary leaning against Joseph, Joseph's arm around her.)

READER *(reading):* "The shepherds said to one another, 'Let's go to Bethlehem and see this thing that has happened, which the Lord has told us about.'" So they hurried off and found Mary and Joseph and the baby, who was lying in the manger.

(Shepherds rise, go to the manger and kneel one by one to look at the baby, then exit left. Spotlight comes up on Reader and lights dim so the stage can be cleared.)

READER *(reading):* "When they had seen him, they spread the word concerning what had been told them about this child, and all who heard it were amazed at what the shepherds said to them. But Mary treasured up all these things and pondered them in her heart. And the shepherds returned, glorifying and praising God for all the things they had heard and seen."

(Light follows Reader off, then full lights come up on Chorus, which has returned to its former position.)

CHORUS: Now to you this may not have seemed much of a
          show,
          Just the same simple story you already know.
          But Jessica, somehow, was touched by the scene,
          And she thought about what that first Christmas
          must mean.

(In above stanza, Jessica remains seated, preoccupied, as parents get coats and put hers on her. Then they walk back

across the stage. She says her lines from near the center before they exit left.)

CHORUS: She asked many questions; she was glad they had come.

JESSICA: Who was this boy Jesus? Where was He from?
What was His mission, that angels would sing?
What is a Savior? What gifts should we bring?

CHORUS: She asked for the story, right from the start.
And like Mary, she pondered these things in her heart.
And when anyone ponders on why Jesus came,
It's certain they won't ever be quite the same.

(For the next two stanzas, lights dim with a spotlight on Chorus, while Jessica's bedroom scene is set stage right.)

CHORUS: For they learn that God cares for us—God loves us so,
And He wanted us surely without doubt to know,
That He asks for our lives and our love in return,
And sent us His Son, that through Him we'd learn.

CHORUS: And that baby Jesus whom shepherds looked for,
Is the same Lord of life who now knocks on the door—
Of our hearts, and keeps asking that we let Him in,
To give us His love and forgive us our sin.

(Lights come up on Jessica propped on one elbow in a robe in bed.)

CHORUS: That night as Jessica lay in her bed,
Some very new thoughts spun around in her head.
That long list of presents was left far behind,
And shepherds, and angels, and stars filled her mind.

(Jessica sits up in bed.)

CHORUS: As she thought of God's kindness in sending His Son,

She tried to remember a kindness she'd done.
But try as she might, she just had to admit,
She thought just of herself and that really was it.

JESSICA: I will change! . . .

CHORUS: . . . she decided,

JESSICA: And I'll take a part,
In doing kind things for people—this morning I'll
start!

CHORUS: And in thinking of others she almost forgot,
About all those presents her parents had bought.

(During the next stanza, Jessica springs out of bed and in a cheerful, excited manner, begins looking around her room.)

CHORUS: So when she got up the next day bright and early,
She wasn't the old Jessie, selfish and surly.
But happy, and giving, and eager, and kind,
She longed to *give* presents; this thought filled her
mind.

(During the next stanza, Jessica speaks, sees paper and crayons, sits at desk and draws.)

JESSICA: What can I give to my mom and dad?

CHORUS: Jessie asked, and with paper and crayons she
had,
She drew them the stable, the manger with hay,
And the star shining bright to show shepherds the
way.

(During the next stanza, Jessica's parents enter her room from right, in robes, and watch her with interest. When Jessica sees them she smiles.)

CHORUS: When Jessica's parents got up, it was late,
For she hadn't yelled out to them, "Don't make me
wait!"
Instead they felt rested, and started the day,
With a smile from the face of their Jessica May.

(During next stanza, Jessica gets up, goes to her parents, kisses them and gives them the picture.)

JESSICA: Merry Christmas! . . .

CHORUS: . . . She said, and she gave them a kiss,
And gave them her art, saying . . .

JESSICA: . . . I made you this.
And I'm sorry for years that I've been such a brat,
And from now on I promise I'm stopping all that.

(During the next stanza, Jessica's parents, delighted, give her a hug as they exit right.)

CHORUS: It was true, she did stop being selfish and greedy,
And started to care for all who were needy.
You know, all it took to change Jessica May,
Was to think of what God did that first Christmas
Day.

Questions for Discussion

1. Why did Jessica like Christmas at the beginning of the play?

2. What was she like at the beginning of the play?

3. What was the play about that Jessica's parents took her to see?

4. What did Jessica think of that play?

5. Why did it make her see herself differently?

6. What did she learn about Jesus?

7. How had Jessica changed by the end of the play?

Sharing

This play, to be acted by five children, illustrates the advantage of sharing and cooperating. When four children hoard the toys, they are very limited in what they can do, but when one child comes up with a creative idea and suggests sharing the toys, the others are motivated to be less selfish. You can change "Christmas gifts" to "birthday gifts" to make this play suitable for any time of year.

Characters

LISA

CRAIG

DALE

KAREN

JASON—(has the most lines).

Costumes

Ordinary clothing.

Props

Four Barbie dolls, four hero-figure dolls (i.e. "Masters of the Universe," "Transformers," whatever is current), a toy race-track in its box, a big box of building blocks, as many rubber insects and dinosaurs as you can muster.

(Lisa enters with four or more Barbie dolls in her hand and addresses audience.)

LISA: I just got another Barbie for Christmas, so now I have four and I'm not going to share them with anyone!

(As each child enters, holding his toys possessively, the others listen to him. Craig enters, with four hero-figure dolls.)

CRAIG: I told everyone I wanted a _____ for Christmas, so now I have four and I'm not going to share them with anyone!

(Dale enters with toy racetrack in its box.)

DALE: Wow, this is the best Christmas present I ever got. I've wanted a racetrack for a long, long time. And now that I've got it, I'm not gonna share it with anybody!

(Karen enters with big box of building blocks.)

KAREN: I got these building blocks for Christmas and they're really great. They're all different shapes and colors and you can make anything you want. Yesterday I made an airplane. Today I'm going to make a big house, and I'm not going to share my blocks with anybody!

(Jason enters, with his arms full of rubber insects and dinosaurs, wiggling all over.)

JASON: My brother got me a whole bunch of these things for Christmas. They're really fun to play with. I put a snake in my sister's bed last night and she screamed! *(Looks at other children.)* Hey, you want to play with them.?

(Others just stare at him. He notices their toys.)

JASON: Hey, you all have neat toys too. Let's play with all of them.

(Others swing away from Jason, pulling their toys even closer.)

ALL: We're not going to share these with anybody!

JASON *(after a pause of surprise, to Lisa):* Don't you get sick of playing with dolls all by yourself?

LISA: Sometimes

JASON *(to Craig):* How can you play with all those things at once?

CRAIG: Well, I just play with them one at a time.

25

JASON *(to Dale):* Don't you ever have races against anyone else?

DALE: I have to pretend my car's racing someone else's.

JASON *(to Karen):* Don't you ever want someone to build something with you?

KAREN: Maybe.

JASON *(thinks for a minute):* I've got an idea of how we could have a lot more fun than playing with toys by ourselves.

LISA: How?

JASON *(excited):* Well, first we could build a big house with the blocks, and that could be the Barbies' house. Then we could set up the racetrack and have a race, and we could pretend the Barbies were watching. Two of them could want one car to win and two could want the other car to win. Then we could make all my snakes and monsters come and attack the Barbies and they could hide in the house and we could have the _____ (hero figures) come and help the Barbies fight the snakes and monsters.

DALE *(enthusiastically):* Hey, that sounds great! *(To others.)* Don't you think so?

(Others agree with enthusiasm.)

DALE: Yeah! I'll share my racetrack so we can do that.

KAREN: And I'll share my blocks.

LISA: And I'll share my dolls.

CRAIG: And I'll share my _____s.

JASON: Great! We can play in my yard. Let's go!

(They quickly exit, eagerly talking.)

Questions for Discussion

1. How were the first four children you saw in the play behaving?

2. How was Jason different from the others?

3. Did it seem like the children who weren't sharing had much fun playing with their toys by themselves?

4. What did Jason want to do?

5. Do you think what he wanted to do was more fun than everyone just playing with their own toys?

6. Why don't we always want to share what we have with others?

7. What must we be very careful to do when people share what is theirs with us?

Basil Is Forgiven

This play is about God's forgiveness and the need for us to forgive one another. It is longer than most of the other plays in this book, and will therefore require more rehearsal time. It also has a set with quite a few props.

This play is ideal for a special presentation, since adults will enjoy it as much as children. It has a festive setting; a party is being prepared, and you can use the set for an actual party including the audience when the play is over. This will give the audience a fun sense of involvement and will justify your work on decorations and food.

The play needs an older narrator who is a good storyteller, a man and a woman to play parents, and five committed children of varying ages. (The two girls can be played by teenagers.) For the sake of humor and continuity, the actors must know their lines and movements precisely, and keep up the pace.

Characters

BASIL—The lead. He plays the youngest child, but you will need at least a third or fourth grader to master the role. He should be cute and convincing.

FREDDIE—Older than Basil.

ERROL—Older than Freddie, high-strung, moves quickly.

CATHERINE—Older than Errol, possibly adolescent. She is milder and kinder than her sister.

ELIZABETH—The eldest, possibly adolescent. She is nasty and snobbish until the end.

NARRATOR—An animated storyteller with a pleasant voice.

FATHER—A convincing adult actor.

MOTHER—She makes a short appearance.

Costumes

Everyone is dressed for a party. The play has an old-fashioned, British feel to it, which can be reflected in clothing. Basil needs to wear a green cap.

Props

The setting is a pleasant living/dining area, with the table upstage left and the living area upstage right. The right exit is to the outside, the left is into the kitchen and the rest of the house.

You will need: a fake snake (or a real one!); a book; a feather duster; a pretty table cloth; a large, gorgeous chocolate cake, decorated as described; other party food, as much as you want; party decorations that actors can quickly put up; a crystal vase with two orchids in it; gift-wrapped boxes; and a piece of paper with writing on it (Catherine's poem).

(Narrator enters and addresses the audience. She will remain to one side of the stage throughout the play. As she begins to speak, Basil enters and stands center.)

NARRATOR: Once upon a time, there lived a little boy named Basil Winthrop who wore a green cap and liked to eat chocolate. Basil came from a big family—he had four brothers and sisters. Basil was the youngest. Then there was Freddie, who kept a snake.

(Freddie enters with snake wrapped around his neck and arms. He continually pets and plays with the snake throughout the play. Freddie bumps Basil to the side, taking central position. This will happen as each sibling enters; displacing the others one step to the side, so Basil ends up being shoved aside four times.)

NARRATOR: Next came Errol, who ran very fast and could not keep still.

(Errol dashes on, bumping into Freddie, who then shoves Basil. Errol stands with his arms folded, always shifting or tapping his feet.)

29

NARRATOR: The second oldest child in the Winthrop family was Catherine, who was always reading a book.

(Catherine enters holding a book in front of her face. Oblivious to her surroundings, she bumps into Errol {who bumps into Freddie, who bumps into Basil}. She staggers and rights herself, closing the book.)

NARRATOR: And the oldest child was Elizabeth, who thought she was very important.

(Elizabeth enters, nose in the air, walks proudly up to Catherine and gives her a deliberate shove, stepping firmly into the central position. Catherine, in turn, shoves Errol, etc. Basil, by this time, is way over to one side of the stage, nursing a bruised shoulder.)

NARRATOR: As you have probably already figured out, Basil, as the youngest child, got shoved around a little. Now the Winthrops had two very nice parents, who weren't home at the time our story begins. On this particular day, all the children were very excited and very busy.

(Everyone but Basil starts bustling around as Narrator continues speaking. Freddie goes down right and pretends to teach his snake tricks. Errol picks up a duster and runs around dusting furniture. Catherine and Elizabeth exit left and return with a tablecloth which they put on the table, then exit again.)

NARRATOR: The children had decided to throw a surprise birthday party for their mother, and had asked their aunt to invite her out for the day. They set to work, doing what they could to make it the best party imaginable. There would be games and tricks and surprises; there would be music and decorations and delicious food. Best of all, there would be a gorgeous cake, that Elizabeth and Catherine had been working on for days.

(The girls reenter with the cake and put it on the table. Everyone gathers around to admire it.)

CATHERINE *(to audience):* This cake is decorated with 200 imported Swiss candies, all placed in perfect rows.

(As the girls talk, Basil gets closer to the cake, his eyes wide with delight. He reaches out to touch it. Elizabeth slaps his hand.)

ELIZABETH: Don't you dare lay a finger on that cake, Basil. It's for the party.

CATHERINE: Basil, you eat too much chocolate anyway.

ELIZABETH: Now leave us alone, Basil, we have a lot of work to do.

(They all resume bustling around.)

NARRATOR: Yes, everyone was working very hard. That is, everyone except Basil, who was quite little and didn't really know what to do. He did try to help his brothers and sisters.

BASIL *(approaching Freddie):* Hey Freddie, whatcha doing?

FREDDIE: I'm teaching my snake party tricks.

BASIL *(stroking the snake):* Can I teach it a trick?

FREDDIE *(exiting right):* Nope. It only listens to me.

(Basil begins following Errol around as he dusts.)

BASIL: Hey, what are you doing, Errol?

ERROL: I'm cleaning up the whole house for Mom. She's going to be really surprised.

BASIL: Could I help you clean up?

ERROL: No, I want to tell her I did it all myself. Besides, you're too slow at everything to be any help.

(Errol exits left and Basil approaches Catherine, who is talking with Elizabeth.)

BASIL: Hey, Catherine, are you getting ready for the party too?

CATHERINE: I certainly am.

BASIL: Could I help you?

CATHERINE: I'm afraid not Basil. *(Exiting left.)* I'm going to write a poem for Mother and I have to be alone.

BASIL *(to Elizabeth):* What about you, Elizabeth? You're the only one left. Could I help you?

ELIZABETH: Not a chance, Basil. I'm going to buy an exquisite crystal vase for the table and two perfect orchids to put in it, for Mother. Glass shops and fine florists are not places for little boys.

(She begins exiting right. Basil looks after her, forlorn.)

BASIL *(plaintively):* Well, what am I going to do for Mommy?

ELIZABETH *(over her shoulder):* How should I know? Draw her a picture.

BASIL *(to audience):* People are always telling little kids to draw pictures.

NARRATOR: Basil was upset. *(Basil crosses his arms and pouts.)* He just didn't feel a part of things at all. The more he thought about how his brothers and sisters were treating him, the madder he got. In fact, he got so mad, he began to want to do something really nasty, just to get back at them. *(Basil's face takes on a mischievous expression.)*

BASIL: I'm going to mess something up!

NARRATOR: Yes, he would mess something up, just to get back at them—just to show them they couldn't shove him around! *(Basil scowls and looks around the room.)* He was just wondering what he could do when his eyes fell on the cake—that gorgeous four-layered chocolate fudge cake with icing made from 5000 chocolate chips, and decorated with Swiss candies in perfect rows. Now, we already know how much Basil liked to eat chocolate. It was his very favorite food. The cake looked so good, and he was so mad at everyone, that Basil made an amazing decision.

BASIL: I'm going to pick off some of the candies! *(He tiptoes* over to the cake and picks off candies, eating one and shoving others in his pockets. His actions continue to follow the narration.)

NARRATOR: That was all he meant to do, but the icing looked so good, that he scooped a little off with his finger and tried it. It tasted so good, he did it again—and again! Then it occurred to him that if the icing was that good, the cake must be wonderful, and before he stopped to think about what an awful thing he was doing, Basil stuck his hand into the middle of the cake and grabbed a big chunk of it! Now this was a bad time for Basil's brothers and sisters to come back, but that's what happened.

(Basil is stuffing cake into his mouth as all brothers and sisters reenter from where they left. Freddie still has his snake and Errol his duster. Catherine holds a piece of paper and Elizabeth a crystal vase with two orchids in it. They all see Basil at once. They all stop and their mouths drop open.)

ALL (at once): Basil! What are you doing?

(Basil tries to answer, but his mouth is full of cake.)

ELIZABETH (approaching the cake): Oh—look what he's done! He's taken the Swiss candies off and messed up the perfect rows!

CATHERINE (approaching the cake): He's licked the icing off!

FREDDIE and ERROL (approaching the cake): He's grabbed a chunk right out of the middle!

(All stand glaring at Basil.)

NARRATOR: They were all very angry at Basil and screamed at him.

ALL (screaming, pointing to the right): Get out of our sight!

(Basil runs down right and cowers. Elizabeth puts down the vase, picks up the cake and they all exit left except Basil.)

33

NARRATOR: Basil's brothers and sisters took the cake into the kitchen, where they did their best to fix it up. This took a long time and stopped them from getting other things done. They were furious with Basil. And Basil, by now, felt terrible. Not only because they were mad at him, but also because he realized that he had spoiled something beautiful that was made for his mom and he had ruined everyone's happiness. Basil was very sorry.

(Brothers and sisters reenter with repaired cake. Basil is still cowering in the corner. As dialogue continues, they bring on other plates of food and put up decorations.)

NARRATOR: He knew he had done a selfish and mean thing, and he didn't want to do a thing like that ever again. He wanted to tell the others how sorry he was.

BASIL *(timidly coming out of his corner):* Hey, everyone, I'm so sorry for messing up the cake. It was a terrible thing to do.

ELIZABETH: Hey—get back to that corner! Don't think you'll get out of this just by saying you're sorry!

BASIL: No, but I really am sorry. I know I did a mean thing.

CATHERINE: You should have thought of that before you started stuffing cake in your mouth!

BASIL: I'm never going to do anything like that again. Did you get the cake fixed up for Mommy?

FREDDIE: Yes, but we're never going to forgive you.

ELIZABETH: Just wait until your father gets home and hears what you've done!

ALL: Yeah!

NARRATOR: At the thought of his father coming, Basil grew even more miserable. He would be so disappointed in him. Basil dreaded the sound of his father's voice at the front door. He didn't have to wait long.

(A man's "hello" is heard off right and Basil shrinks further into his corner. Father appears with an armload of presents, moves to center, and looks around, smiling.)

FATHER: Well, everything looks great. Are we all ready for the party?

ELIZABETH: Well we would be, Father, if it weren't for Basil. *(Jerks her head towards the corner.)*

FATHER: Oh? *(Puts gifts on a chair.)*

CATHERINE: Basil has done an awful thing.

ERROL: A mean thing.

FREDDIE: A selfish thing.

FATHER *(approaches Basil):* What did you do, Basil?

BASIL *(eyes downcast):* Oh Dad, I messed up Mommy's cake. I took off the candies and licked the icing and . . . and ate a chunk out of it.

FATHER: I'm so surprised at you. Your sisters worked so hard on that cake. Why did you do that?

BASIL: I was mad at them for leaving me out, but I'm not mad now—I'm very sorry.

FREDDIE: He keeps saying that, but we've already told him we're never going to forgive him.

(Father looks from Basil to Freddie, sizing up the situation.)

FATHER *(after a pause):* You say you're never going to forgive him?

FREDDIE: Nope. Never.

FATHER: And what about the rest of you?

ALL *(shaking their heads):* Never.

ELIZABETH: Certainly not. He's a terrible child. I'm ashamed he's my brother.

FATHER *(looking disappointed, a little angry):* Then don't you see that you are as much in the wrong as Basil? Freddie, when you frightened that little girl next door so badly with your snake, did I forgive you?

FREDDIE: Yeah, you did.

FATHER: Errol, did I forgive you when you played with your basketball inside and broke the china cups?

ERROL: Oh yeah, You did.

FATHER: Catherine, what did I say to you when I found out you cheated on that important test in school?

CATHERINE: You said I had to tell the teacher, and you forgave me.

FATHER: And Elizabeth, when I found out that you spent all the money I gave you for schoolbooks on clothes, what did I do?

ELIZABETH: You forgave me.

NARRATOR: When the young Winthrops remembered all those wrong things they had done, and they remembered that their kind father had forgiven them, they felt guilty. They realized they had often done worse things than Basil.

FATHER *(approaching Basil)*: Well Basil, you know I have to punish you. So you won't be having any more of this cake, or any chocolate for a while, but I forgive you. We'll pretend this never happened.

BASIL *(smiling)*: OK.

FATHER: And you others, since you have been forgiven so many time, what do you think you should do?

FREDDIE *(approaching Basil)*: I forgive you, Basil, and I'm sorry I didn't let you help train my snake.

ERROL *(approaching Basil)*: I forgive you, Basil. I'm sorry I didn't let you help me clean up.

CATHERINE *(approaching Basil)*: I forgive you, Basil. I'm sorry I didn't pay more attention to you.

ELIZABETH *(approaching Basil)*: I forgive you, and I'm sorry I said such mean things to you.

FATHER: Well that settles that!

(A woman's "hello" is heard off right.)

FATHER: Quick, she's home!

(They quickly shuffle into a group upstage from right entrance. When Mother enters, they all shout, "Surprise!" Mother gives a delighted reaction. Narrator moves to the center as the actors move over to the table, quietly ad-libbing conversation in the background.)

NARRATOR: And so it turned out to be a wonderful party after all, because Basil was forgiven. And in the same way that Basil had a father who forgave him, our Father God forgives us. And so we should also forgive one another. Well, now that Basil is forgiven and everyone is happy, let's have a party!

(The audience joins the actors on stage for a party.)

Questions for Discussion

1. What place did Basil have in the family?

2. How did Basil's brothers and sisters treat him when he asked to help them get ready for the party?

3. What did Basil do that was wrong?

4. Why did he do it—how was he feeling?

5. How did he feel after he did it?

6. How did his brothers and sisters treat him when they found out?

7. How did his father treat him when he found out?

8. What did the father have to say to Basil's brothers and sisters?

9. How is the father in this play like God?

When You're Scared

This play is quite flexible; you can use as many children as you wish or as few as four. There are few children's speaking parts, and they are small. A larger requirement of the children is the mime they perform throughout the play. You can make this as disciplined and detailed as you want, or keep it quite simple. The dialogue is carried by the teacher, a teenager or adult, who has much to memorize.

The play's aim is to teach children that when they are afraid they can call on the Lord. This is stressed by giving examples of Biblical characters whom God helped when they were afraid.

Before you present the play, discuss with the children what kinds of situations make them afraid, and have them tell those to the audience after the teacher's introduction.

Characters
TEACHER—A lively, eloquent person.

RODNEY, SAMANTHA, and as many other children as you like.

Costumes
Clothing that allows children freedom of movement.

Props
None.

The play begins with the teacher making an announcement.

TEACHER: Good evening/morning/afternoon. Today/tonight we're going to present a play about what to do when you're afraid. But first, the children are going to share with you some situations in which they have been afraid.

(Children are on stage in a casually arranged group. Some can be sitting, some standing. One by one they share with the audience. Have them keep it to one sentence, such as "I'm afraid if someone shuts my door all the way when I'm in bed at night." To end this time with a touch of humor, you could have the last child say something like, "I'm afraid of talking to big groups of people!")

TEACHER: Well, you can see that everyone has something that scares them, and not only kids, but grown-ups too—and even really brave people.

SAMANTHA: Brave people too?

TEACHER: Oh yes. Being brave doesn't mean you don't get scared. The Bible tells all kinds of stories about men who were really frightened, but learned what to do about being afraid. Do you know what they did?

RODNEY: What?

TEACHER: They told God that they were scared, and they asked for His help, and He gave them the strength to do whatever they had to do. Do you want to hear about some of them?

CHILDREN: Yeah!

(Children get into a line or some other orderly form. They stand in straight, attentive positions, looking at the teacher, ready to get involved in the stories, which they will do actions to. When they have no movements to do, they focus on the teacher. The lines now become rhymes.)

TEACHER: We'll start with Moses, who for forty long years
Led sheep through his pastures till one day he hears
God's voice, in a bush, as it burned speaking through it;
"You must save my people; you, Moses, must do it!"

(On the third line above, the children cup hands to ears, listening. On fourth line, they make astonished expressions.)

TEACHER: The people of God were in quite a bad fix,
             And Moses would have to use several tricks,
             To free them from Egypt, where they'd become
                 slaves;
             You'd shudder to see how a Pharaoh behaves.

(On the second line, all children get into cowering positions except one, who on the third line mimes brandishing a whip and whipping the others.)

TEACHER: Now Moses was shy, and he spoke with a stut-
                 ter,
             The thought of this task made his heart melt like
                 butter.
             His fear was so great he gave every excuse,
             He said, "Lord, is there somebody else you
                 could choose?"

(For the first two lines, the children look weak and afraid; on the third line they shake their heads "no" while pointing to themselves. On the last line they mime the words the teacher speaks, or all speak them together. After each rhyming story is over, the children relax into more passive, listening positions as the teacher talks with them.)

TEACHER: Boys and girls, if you were a quiet man who always kept to himself and suddenly, when you were eighty years old, God told you to go into a strange country and some- how lead thousands and thousands of people to escape from it, what would you say?

CHILDREN: Lord, help! I'm scared!

TEACHER: Well, you can bet Moses said that too! But do you know what happened?

CHILDREN: What?

TEACHER: The Lord promised that He would always be with Moses and would teach him what to say and what to do. Moses went to Egypt, and God did all kinds of miracles there to help him, and Moses got all the Israelites out of Egypt—60,000 men plus even more women and children.

And after they left Egypt, they had some very exciting adventures, and Moses was their leader until he died.

CHILDREN: Wow!

TEACHER: Now I'll tell you another story. . . .

(Children return to attentive positions.)

TEACHER: Years later, God's people—in trouble again—
Had lost all their land to the Midianite men.
It was just as bad as when they had been
    slaves;
They'd run out of food and were hiding in caves.

(On the third line, the children pull both corners of their mouths down in exaggerated frowns. On the fourth line, they cup their hands in begging positions, then bend down and cover their heads with their hands in hiding positions.)

TEACHER: And God spoke again, this time to a man,
Very young, very weak and the least of his clan.
He said, "Gideon, you are the man that I
    choose,
To drive out the Midianites. Go, you can't lose!"

(For the last two lines, all the children point to one child, singled out as Gideon, who looks around bewildered.)

TEACHER: Now Gideon thought God was surely mistaken.
To trust him, just wasn't a chance to be taken!
He felt he was even too wimpy to try it,
But God wanted him and he couldn't deny it.

(For all four lines, the children focus on Gideon, who dubiously flexes his muscles, one arm at a time, feeling them with the other hand. On the last line he gives an exaggerated shrug. Then the children relax back into listening positions.)

TEACHER: Boys and girls, if you thought you were a weak and unimportant person, as Gideon seems to have thought, and one day God said that He wanted you to attack those thousands and thousands of Midianites, and with only 300 of your own men, what would you say?

CHILDREN: Lord, help! I'm scared!

TEACHER: Well you can bet Gideon said that too! But do you know what happened?

CHILDREN: What?

TEACHER: God proved to Gideon, three different times in three different ways, that He was going to make the Midianites lose and run away if Gideon attacked them. So finally Gideon led his army to where they were, and sure enough, the Israelites blew their trumpets and shouted and charged —and the Midianites were so scared they ran away! And for years after that, Gideon ruled over God's people.

CHILDREN: Wow!

TEACHER: And I'll tell you one more story. This one happened when the Lord Jesus was living on the earth.

(Children snap back to attentive positions.)

TEACHER: Now evening had settled in Galilee,
But crowds were still down on the shore by the sea.
Jesus taught them for hours until daylight had died,
Then He said, "Let's sail on to the sea's other side."

(For all lines, one child becomes Jesus teaching while the others listen, then on the last line they all mime getting into a boat. If necessary, this move can carry over into the next stanza.)

TEACHER: But as the safe sight of the shore disappeared,
There came just the thing the disciples most feared.
The wind whipped the waves up so fierce and so high,
The disciples were sure they were all going to die.

(As soon as they are all seated, they shield their eyes and look out at the audience, except Jesus, who lies down and goes to sleep. On the third line, they begin to rock back and forth in unison, finding it hard to keep their balance.)

TEACHER: They were cold, they were scared, they were
        probably weeping,
    But Jesus just lay in the boat soundly sleeping!
    While they panicked He slept as if in His own
        bed.
    "Don't you care if we drown?" they woke Him
        and said.

(They get more upset as the stanza goes on, and can say a few ad-libbed lines, such as "Help" and "We're drowning," but take care not to let them distract from the narration. Finally they shake Jesus awake, and either mime what the narrator says or say it together. Then they relax and draw closer to the teacher to listen again.)

TEACHER: Boys and girls, if you were in a little tiny boat in the middle of the sea and you were caught by a terrible storm that tossed your boat so that it nearly tipped over, and the waves were breaking over it and filling it up with water, what would you say?

CHILDREN: Lord, help! I'm scared!

TEACHER: Well you can bet the disciples said that too! But do you know what happened?

CHILDREN: What?

TEACHER: When the disciples woke the Lord up, and it looked as if nothing could stop that awful storm, Jesus got up, and simply said, "Quiet! Be still!" The wind died down, and it was calm, right away! Then the disciples began to understand just how powerful the Lord really is!

CHILDREN: Wow!

(Teacher goes back to her seat and the children sit around her as at first.)

44

TEACHER: So you see, when something happens to make you afraid, you don't have to let it worry and frighten you so much that you just can't stand it; you can tell the Lord and ask Him to help you. So next time you are scared of anything at all—what will you say?

CHILDREN: Lord, help! I'm scared!

TEACHER: Right! Remember that the Lord is always with you and will always help you.

(Children ad-lib, "We will" etc. as they exit.)

Questions for Discussion

1. What sorts of things were the children afraid of?

2. What had God asked Moses to do? (Story in Exodus 3)

3. What had God asked Gideon to do? (Story in Judges 6 and 7)

4. What happened to Jesus' disciples when they were in the boat? (Story in Mark 4)

5. Were these people scared? What did they do about it? Did God help them?

6. What did the teacher tell the children to do when they were scared?

7. What sort of things are you afraid of? What can you do when you're afraid?

The Battle
of the Thoughts

This play is about the conflict of good and evil within us. Two armies, the Good Thoughts and the Bad Thoughts, engage in verbal and physical battles with one another. Children make up the armies and there is a teenage or adult narrator. The number of children needed is flexible; armies need equal numbers, with a minimum of four or five in each.

The aim of the play is to illustrate the conflict between good and bad that takes place in our minds; flesh versus spirit. By making the conflict clear, children should see the need to respond to right and ignore wrong impulses. Adults will also enjoy this play.

Characters

NARRATOR—A teenager or adult.

KRISTEN—A girl who gives a short monologue.

ALAN—A boy who gives a short monologue.

ARMIES—A good army and an evil army, with three speaking parts in each. The leader of each army should be a child who can act aggressively and speak with confidence.

Costumes

Each army dresses distinctly and uniformly. What they wear is up to your imagination; anything from costumes of medieval fencers to street gangs to "Star Wars" storm troopers; or as simple as black and white shirts. Keep in mind that swords, and belts to hold them, have to fit in somewhere.

Props

A cardboard sword and sheath for each army member.

Narrator enters and stands to one side of the stage, where he or she remains throughout the play.

NARRATOR: Everyone knows that to please God and to be happy, we need to be kind to each other, and be good instead of bad. The problem is that it isn't always easy, is it? Have you ever noticed how sometimes you have thoughts about being good and other thoughts about being bad, almost at the same time? Like when your mom asks you to help her around the house. Some thoughts tell you you should help her and other thoughts tell you you just don't feel like it.

And isn't it true that sometimes the good thoughts win and you do what's right, and sometimes the bad thoughts win and you do what's wrong? Why, it's almost like there was a battle going on right inside your head! Take Kristen, for example.

(Kristen enters and addressed the audience.)

KRISTEN *(looking worried)*: Oh, I don't know what to do. Grandma asked me over to stay at her house a long time ago and I said I would go, but Lisa just asked me to a party on the same day and I want to go to the party more. Grandma has made plans for us and she's really excited about me coming, but I really want to go to Lisa's.

(She exits as Narrator speaks.)

NARRATOR: I'll bet there's a fight going on in Kristen's head right now!

(Good Thoughts enter from the right and stand proudly, arms folded and legs apart. They look brave and heroic. Their leader stands at the front.)

GOOD LEADER *(in a cartoon super-hero voice)*: We are Kristen's good thoughts! We want to love all people and obey the Lord Jesus!

(Bad Thoughts enter left and stand in the same manner. They look evil and threatening. Their leader stands at the front.)

BAD LEADER *(with an evil voice):* We are Kristen's bad thoughts and we don't care about anyone but ourselves. *(Laughs nastily.)*

(Both groups swing to face one another, in unison, remembering to remain half facing the audience. As one member of any army speaks, the others react, agree or ad-lib appropriately.)

GOOD LEADER: Bad Thoughts, get out of Kristen's head! She knows that she should go to her Grandma's house!

BAD LEADER: Aha! But she wants to go to Lisa's *very* much!

GOOD THOUGHT #2: She knows that her Grandma already bought tickets to the circus—she wouldn't let her down.

GOOD THOUGHT #3: Yeah, and Kristen loves her Grandma; she wouldn't disappoint her.

BAD THOUGHT #2: But she also knows that Lisa's party is going to be *great!* Lisa has a really neat house, all her friends are going to be there, and it's a slumber party!

GOOD THOUGHT #3: Well, Kristen knows she promised her Grandma first, and a promise is a promise!

BAD LEADER: That's what you think, Good Thoughts! But we know better. We know Kristen is more worried about missing out on the fun than hurting her Grandma's feelings. We're going to iron you out—ATTACK!

(Both armies draw swords and run at one another. As they are equally matched, they break into separate sword fights, spread all over the stage. Have the battles planned so the Bad Thoughts get the Good Thoughts pinned to the ground one by one until they are all down. Let the children choreograph their own fights but within the time and space you give them. The leaders fight one another and finish last, and when the Good Leader is finally pinned, Bad Leader puts his foot on Good Leader's chest and raises his fist in triumph.)

BAD LEADER: Bad Thoughts have the victory! Kristen will go to the party and forget her Grandma!

(Bad Thoughts shout "Hooray," "Yippee," etc. as they put away their swords and exit left. As they leave, Good Thoughts get up slowly and walk off right, dejectedly and silently, Good Leader addresses them.)

GOOD LEADER: Never give up, Troops.

NARRATOR: Yes, sometimes the bad thoughts win. Now, let's take a look at Alan, and see what's going on in his mind.

ALAN: Boy, have I ever got a problem. I don't know what I'm going to do. All my best friends—Bobby and Michael and Ken—have made up this secret club, and they want me to be in it. And I really want to, but to get in the club you have to do something wrong like steal, or let the air out of someone's tires, or throw rocks at windows, and I don't want to do that. I know that's wrong, but I don't want to be the only one left out. *(Exits as he speaks.)* I just don't know what I'm going to do. . . .

(After he exits, the armies reenter and stand as before.)

GOOD LEADER: We are Alan's good thoughts! We want to love all people and obey the Lord Jesus!

BAD LEADER: We are Alan's bad thoughts! We don't care about anyone but ourselves! *(Laughs nastily.)*

(They swing around to confront one another, as before.)

BAD LEADER: You don't have a chance this time, Good Thoughts! All of Alan's best friends are in that group, and there's no way he'd have the guts to tell them they're wrong!

GOOD LEADER: Don't be so sure, Bad Thoughts! Alan has always known that it is wrong to steal and wreck other people's things!

BAD THOUGHT #2: So what? Do you think he's going to be left behind while the other three go on all kinds of adventures?

GOOD THOUGHT #2: If he has to, yes! He knows if they were good friends they wouldn't leave him behind anyway!

BAD THOUGHT #3: Ha! Do you think that just because his parents tell him that he's going to believe it?

GOOD LEADER: Yes we do, Bad Thoughts! Alan cares more about doing the right thing than being in the gang, and there's nothing you can do about it. ATTACK!!!

(The battle proceeds as before, only this time the Good Thoughts pin down the Bad Thoughts, the leader falling last of all. Good Leader puts his foot on Bad Leader's chest and raises his fist in triumph.)

GOOD LEADER: Well done, Good Thoughts! We have won and Alan will not hurt anyone or anything to get into the club!

(Good Thoughts shout "Hooray," "Yippee," etc. as they exit right. Bad Thoughts struggle up slowly and shuffle off dejectedly by the left exit. Bad Leader addresses them.)

BAD LEADER: Hey Guys, don't worry. We'll try again soon.

NARRATOR: Yes, sometimes the bad thoughts win and sometimes the good thoughts win. But there is something that you need to remember. If you keep listening to your bad thoughts, it gets easier and easier to let them win and cause you to do wrong. But if you ask the Lord to help you and make you strong, then you will be able to listen to your good thoughts and it will get easier and easier for them to win and cause you to do right. So which thoughts are you going to listen to?

Questions for Discussion

1. What are the two armies that are fighting for control of our action?

2. What did Kristen have to make a choice about?

3. What did she decide? Did she listen to her bad thoughts or her good thoughts?

4. What did Alan have to make a choice about?

5. What did he decide? Did he listen to his bad thoughts or his good thoughts?

6. Can you think of some good thoughts and some bad thoughts that you have had?

7. What happens if we listen to our bad thoughts?

8. What happens when we listen to our good thoughts.

9. When we know we should listen to our good thoughts, but we just don't feel like we can, who can we ask to help us?

Zaccheus
the Tax Collector

This play can be performed by children but the narrator must be a teenager or an adult. The narrator stands to one side of the stage and tells most of the story as the children act it out. Except for a few comments from the crowd, Zaccheus and Jesus are the only characters with speaking parts. The aim of this play is to illustrate, through the story of Zaccheus in Luke 19:1-9, Jesus' love for those who are rejected by others. This play can be presented to adults too.

Characters

ZACCHEUS—Pick a child with the ability to demonstrate emotions and memorize lines.

TALL PEOPLE—Three children significantly taller than Zaccheus, They can also be part of the crowd or disciples.

JESUS—Pick a child who can say lines without sounding stilted.

CROWD—Six to twelve children who can sustain an interest in their expectancy of Jesus.

TREE—Two taller, older people who can stand still.

DISCIPLES—Any number of children who will follow Jesus on and off stage.

Costumes
Biblical costumes. Zaccheus is dressed better than the rest.

Props
A briefcase, a stool or hassock.

Narrator enters and takes position.

NARRATOR: During the time when Jesus walked on the earth, there was a man named Zaccheus, who lived in Jericho.

(Three tall people enter, who walk across the stage in single file in order of height. Zaccheus follows a little farther behind and stops center stage and faces the audience. He is carrying a briefcase.)

NARRATOR: Zaccheus was a very short man. He was also a very rich man. *(Zaccheus opens his briefcase to reveal stacks of $1000 bills.)* He was also a tax collector. Now at that time, a tax collector was not a very popular person, and was treated very badly.

(The tall people reenter and pass behind Zaccheus, insulting him.)

TALL PERSON #1: Scum.

TALL PERSON #2: Low life.

TALL PERSON #3: You crummy little cheat.

(Zaccheus looks after them with a hurt expression.)

NARRATOR: Now Zaccheus may have deserved *some* of these insults, but he didn't deserve all of them. People liked to pick on Zaccheus and call him a sinner. Sometimes people pick on others and try to make them seem really bad just so they can feel better about themselves. That's what people did to Zaccheus back in Jericho 2000 years ago. One day, a huge crowd gathered on the street in Jericho where Zaccheus lived.

(Crowd enters and stands close, blocking Zaccheus from view. Two people also form a tree, standing back to back behind the crowd and forming branches with their arms. A stool or hassock is moved behind them out of view, so that when Zaccheus stands on it, he is elevated and can peek through the "branches." The crowd is talking excitedly.)

NARRATOR: Zaccheus tried hard to find out what was going on, but when you are really short, it's hard to see in a crowd.

(Zaccheus' face appears as he jumps up behind people, trying to see over them. Finally, he tugs someone's sleeve and pushes his head between two people.)

NARRATOR: Finally he got someone's attention.

ZACCHEUS: What's going on?

CROWD MEMBER: Don't you know? Jesus is in town.

ZACCHEUS: Jesus? of Nazareth?

CROWD MEMBER: Yeah, He's coming this way. Now get out of my way. *(He pushes Zaccheus out of the way, so he disappears back behind the crowd again.)*

NARRATOR: Now Zaccheus was very anxious to see Jesus. Like the rest of the crowd, he had heard stories about this man; how He was a wonderful teacher, how He made sick people well and even did miracles like stopping a storm on the lake just by saying, "Be still." Most of the crowd was wondering if Jesus would do anything like that in Jericho. For some reason, just the thought of seeing Jesus gave Zaccheus a happy, excited feeling inside. But how was he ever going to see Jesus if the crowd didn't let him through? But then Zaccheus got an idea! He looked around and saw a fig tree nearby. Fig trees have good strong branches and are easy to climb, so Zaccheus scrambled up the tree. *(Zaccheus appears elevated above the crowd, peeking through the tree branches.)*

NARRATOR: Another thing about fig trees is that they have big soft leaves, and Zaccheus figured he could get a good view of Jesus but the leaves would hide him so no one could see him and pick on him. He had just settled down in the crook of a branch when someone in the crowd called out:

VOICE #1: Hey, here He comes!

(The crowd begins to murmur louder and show more excitement. Jesus enters, followed by His disciples.)

NARRATOR: Jesus stopped in front of the crowd. *(Jesus stops.)* Zaccheus looked down at Him and expected Him to begin teaching, or asking if there were any sick people who needed healing, but Jesus did neither of these things. What He did do gave Zaccheus the surprise of his life. Jesus knew Zaccheus by name, and He knew he was up in the fig tree!

(Jesus looks up at Zaccheus.)

JESUS: Zaccheus, come down right away. I must stay at your house today.

ZACCHEUS *(with a big smile):* Me? My house?

(Jesus smiles back and nods. The crowd watches with surprise and disapproval. Zaccheus scrambles down from the tree and emerges from the crowd. When he reaches Jesus, Jesus puts His arm around his shoulders.)

NARRATOR: Now when the crowd saw Jesus walking off with the most hated man in the town, they were very angry. They didn't understand that Jesus cared just as much about Zaccheus as He did about the important people who everyone liked, and that He had some special things He wanted to teach Zaccheus.

VOICE #2: Hey, how come if Jesus is so famous, He's spending His time with someone like the Tax Collector?

VOICE #3: Yeah, doesn't He know what kind of rotten person he is?

VOICE #4: Why's He ignoring all the important people and eating with that little scum.

(Everyone except the disciples begin to exit, but Jesus stops them.)

JESUS: Wait! *(All stop exiting and look back at Jesus.)* I haven't come to call the righteous, but sinners to repentance. . . . Come on, Zaccheus.

(All watch as Jesus and Zaccheus exit together, Jesus' arm around Zaccheus. They hold their positions, looking offstage, as Narrator concludes.)

NARRATOR: So you see, even though Jesus didn't do any miracles in Jericho that day. He did a very important thing. He showed the people of Jericho that He loved a man whom everyone else hated. He wanted those people to know that He loved everyone—and He wants everyone who hears this story to know the same thing.

Questions for Discussion

1. Why did people pick on Zaccheus?

2. Is there anyone like Zaccheus at your school—someone who the other kids pick on?

3. Why did everyone in Jericho want to see Jesus?

4. Why did Zaccheus climb up in the fig tree?

5. What did Jesus say to Zaccheus when He met him?

6. Did Jesus treat Zaccheus the same as the other people in the play?

7. Why did Jesus treat him the way He did? (i.e. How did Jesus feel about Zaccheus?)

8. How should we treat people others are unkind to?

Gossiping

This short play illustrates how damaging and misleading gossip can be. It involves conversations between four girls. All girls have quite a few lines, especially Debbie. The play can be adapted for boys with a few line changes.

Characters
TANYA—A new girl.

DEBBIE—The main character.

MANDY—A gossip.

SUSAN—A girl who doesn't gossip.

Costumes
Ordinary school clothing.

Props
The girls can carry books and lunch boxes, since they are on their way home from school. Debbie needs to have a new looking Barbie doll.

Tanya enters left, walking slowly. Debbie enters right and they meet center and stop.

DEBBIE: Hi. You're new here, aren't you?

TANYA: Yeah.

DEBBIE: Do you think you'll like our school?

TANYA: Well, I guess so, but I like my other school better because all my friends are there and I don't have any here.

DEBBIE: Well, I'll be your friend. Want to see my Barbie? *(Or whatever the current popular doll is.)*

TANYA: Yeah. Is she new?

DEBBIE *(getting the doll from her bag):* Uh-huh. I got her for my birthday.

TANYA: Hey—I just got that one too! She's my favorite.

DEBBIE: Mine too. You know, I've got a big house for my dolls. Maybe you could come over and see it.

TANYA: Yeah, that would be fun. Let's ask our moms today.

DEBBIE: OK, I'll see you tomorrow then. You can play with us at recess.

TANYA: Thanks—bye!

(Tanya exits right as Mandy enters left. Mandy approaches Debbie.)

MANDY: Hey Debbie, were you just talking to that new girl?

DEBBIE: Yeah, she's going to be my friend.

MANDY: What? You're going to be friends with her?

DEBBIE: Yeah. Why not?

MANDY: Well, I'd never be her friend in a million years.

DEBBIE: How come?

MANDY: Because she's dumb. She sits near me and I can see her work. She can't do math at all.

DEBBIE: Can't she?

MANDY: Nope. And at recess, someone asked her if she wanted a turn on the monkey bars and she couldn't spin around or anything. You can just tell she's dumb. And a crybaby. She was crying at lunchtime for no reason.

DEBBIE: Oh. Well I didn't know she was like that.

MANDY: Well she is. Anyway, I have to get home. See you later.

DEBBIE: Bye.

(Debbie stands thinking a moment as Mandy exits right and

Susan enters right, saying "Hi" to Mandy as they pass. Susan approaches Debbie.)

SUSAN: Hi, Debbie, how are you?

DEBBIE: OK. Have you met the new girl at school?

SUSAN: Yeah. I sat next to her in reading.

DEBBIE: Mandy says she's a real dummy.

SUSAN: What? She's not dumb. She was reading harder books than anyone else in the class.

DEBBIE: Oh. Well, Mandy said she can't do math.

SUSAN: Maybe it's different math from what she was doing in her old school.

DEBBIE: Oh. Well she's no fun to play with. She can't even spin on the monkey bars.

SUSAN: So what? Maybe she didn't have monkey bars at her other school. What does it matter? She played with us today and we all had fun.

DEBBIE: Well I do know she's a crybaby. She was crying today for no reason.

SUSAN: How do you know?

DEBBIE: Mandy told me.

SUSAN: What does Mandy know? No one cries for no reason. It's scary going to a new school. There's lots of reasons she could have been crying. Debbie, why do you listen to gossip? Mandy doesn't know anything about Tanya.

DEBBIE *(pauses):* Yeah. You're right.

SUSAN: I thought Tanya was really nice.

DEBBIE: I thought that too—then Mandy changed my mind. I'm glad I talked to you. I better not listen to gossip anymore—I nearly lost a friend for no reason at all.

Questions for Discussion

1. What is gossip?

2. What did Debbie think of Tanya at the beginning of the play?

3. What did Mandy say about Tanya?

4. Did Mandy change Debbie's opinion of Tanya?

5. What did Debbie realize when she talked to Susan?

6. What do you think would have happened if Debbie had not talked with Susan after she talked to Mandy?

7. Should Debbie have listened to Mandy's gossip?

8. Can you think of a time when gossip has hurt someone?

Following Jesus

This play about Jesus' disciples shows that while they failed Him many times, with His help they were able to follow Him and continue His work after He left. This play relies on the narrator to hold interest, and on the children to perform their actions with precision. They don't have many lines, but the action must be well rehearsed. Have as many children as you wish for disciples, preferably an even number with a minimum of six.

Characters

NARRATOR—A good storyteller, who will also be part of the action as a Jesus figure.

DISCIPLES—As many children as you want.

Costumes

Disciples should wear the usual New Testament garb: robes, sandals, headdresses. Don't worry about being too realistic and don't be afraid of color.

Props

None.

The play begins with the disciples spread all over the stage miming different occupations. Several of them can be fishing; casting nets and pulling them in, with some in a boat and the others on the shore. Others can pretend to be writing at desks, picking grapes, cutting wheat, selling something. None of them make any noise. Narrator enters and speaks from one side of the stage.

NARRATOR: While Jesus was living on the earth, He had a group of followers, disciples, who went with Him wherever He went. These people had all been working at different jobs until they met Jesus.

(All disciples freeze and look at Narrator.)

NARRATOR: But after they met Jesus, they left their jobs and their homes and everything behind to follow Him.

(Disciples break freeze, mime dropping what they are doing suddenly, and line up behind Narrator in a straight line.)

NARRATOR: Even though these disciples loved Jesus very much, and had been willing to leave everything to follow Him, they failed Him an awful lot.

(Disciples look at audience and nod.)

NARRATOR: They would follow Him to hear Him tell stories with a special meaning, called parables . . .

(Disciples quickly gather around Narrator. They freeze in listening positions as Narrator freezes for a few seconds in a teaching position before resuming narration.)

NARRATOR: . . . But they couldn't understand what the parables meant.

(Disciples scratch their heads and look at the audience and each other with puzzled expressions.)

NARRATOR: They followed Him to a grassy hillside where thousands of needy people had gathered to hear His teaching.

(As Narrator speaks, he circles around half the stage, disciples filing behind, stops off center and disciples stop in a straight row, all facing audience.)

NARRATOR: . . . And though they had seen God do wonderful miracles already, when Jesus told them that five loaves of bread and two fishes would feed all those people, they didn't believe Him.

(Disciples cross arms and shake heads from side to side, all at the same time.)

DISCIPLES: It can't be done!

NARRATOR: But of course you know it was done. . . . They followed Him from town to town . . .

(Narrator walks in a figure eight around the stage as he speaks, disciples following.)

NARRATOR: . . . To Galilee and Capernaum, to the hill country and across the lake, to the villages on the shore, to Tyre, to Sidon, to the Sea of Galilee, and to the region of the Decapolis. They followed Him to Bethsaida, to Caesarea Philippi, into Judea, across the Jordan, and finally to Jerusalem.

(Narrator stops at the spot where he began, and the disciples freeze, looking at one another in pairs.)

NARRATOR: They followed Him as He went to all those places and watched Him humbly serving people—and then on their way, they argued about which one of them was the greatest!

(Disciples argue with each other, shouting "I'm the greatest," "No, I am," etc. until Narrator makes a motion to cease.)

NARRATOR: They followed Him among crowds of little children, who Jesus loved and wanted to bless. . . .

(Disciples make a protective circle around Narrator, facing outwards, frowning and holding out their arms as if to stop children from approaching.)

NARRATOR: But they didn't understand, and thought their leader was too important to stop for the children, so they tried to keep the children from Him.

(Narrator ducks out of the circle the disciples have formed, and the disciples huddle tightly together and kneel, as if sitting in a boat.)

NARRATOR: One disciple even followed Jesus when He walked on the water. . . .

(One disciple cautiously steps out of the boat as the Narrator passes.)

DISCIPLE: Lord, tell me to come with You!

NARRATOR *(holding out his hand):* Come.

(Disciple mimes walking a few hesitant steps with eyes on Narrator.)

NARRATOR: But when he looked down *(Disciple looks down.)* and saw the water, he lost faith that the Lord could keep him going, and started to sink.

(Disciple sinks to his knees with a frightened expression.)

DISCIPLE: Lord, save me!

(Narrator grabs his hand and pulls him up. Others stand.)

NARRATOR *(in a more serious tone):* Yes, the disciples failed Jesus many, many times. The day before He was crucified, they followed Him to the Garden of Gethsemane, and in His loneliest hour, when His enemies came to take Him away. . .

(Two disciples seize Narrator by the arms and hold him, while the others back away in fear.)

NARRATOR: . . . They left Him all alone.

(After a pause, Narrator picks up a Bible from nearby, or someone hands him one.)

NARRATOR: But even though Jesus knew His disciples would fail Him, He still loved them and wanted them to be His followers. Listen to what He said to them *(Reads.):* "I am the vine; you are the branches. If you remain in me and I in you, you will bear much fruit; apart from me you can do nothing" (John 25:5).

(Disciples drift back on stage.)

NARRATOR: So the disciples learned that they could follow Him only if they leaned on the Lord's help and strength. Once they learned that, even after He had gone back to Heaven, they kept doing what Jesus had done.

DISCIPLE #1: Teaching people,

DISCIPLE #2: Showing people God's power,

DISCIPLE #3: Serving people without worrying about who's the greatest,

ALL: And loving one another!

(Disciples hug one another.)

NARRATOR *(to audience):* And the Lord wants us to put our failures behind us, and live the same way!

(Disciples follow Narrator offstage.)

Questions for Discussion

1. What did the disciples do when they met Jesus?

2. After they met Jesus, did the disciples always live just like Jesus did?

3. In what ways did the disciples fail Jesus: a) When He taught them, b) When He was feeding the 5000 people, c) When His enemies came to take Him away?

4. What were the disciples arguing about at one point? Why would this make Jesus sad?

5. How did Jesus treat little children? How did the disciples treat little children?

6. Why did one disciple start sinking after he started to walk on the water with Jesus?

7. Did Jesus stop loving His disciples after they failed Him?

8. What did Jesus teach the disciples at the end of the play?

9. What could they do if they learned this lesson?

Jericho Falls

This story, from Joshua 5 and 6, is told by an adult narrator and acted out by the children. It is a play in which you can involve many children, and only Joshua and the messenger have lines to learn. All the other children have to do is march back and forth across the stage and make a lot of noise at the right time.

In retelling the story of the wall of Jericho falling, the aim is to give the children an example of the power of God.

Characters

NARRATOR—An adult.

JOSHUA—A convincing actor.

MESSENGER

ISRAELITES—As many children as you can muster, including a troop of guards, seven priests with horns (or less if you have a smaller group), and the rest of the people.

Costumes

Consult Bible pictures. Something like short white tunics draped over one shoulder with loose belts and sandals would be suitable for the guards. Joshua can wear a headdress or a cape to suggest leadership. The Messenger of God should also wear a white cape (and anything else you can think of to make him look impressive). The priests can wear choir robes and the rest of the people can wear various long, loose clothes and sandals, with girls covering their heads with scarves.

Props

A sword for the messenger, seven rams' horns for the priests, (they can be fake with the noise coming from brass instruments offstage). And a wall of Styrofoam or cardboard boxes.

The wall is made of equally sized boxes painted to look like stones. The wall is upstage (back, away from the audience), as high and wide as you can make it. Tie strings around several of the foundation boxes and trail them offstage, so when the time comes for the wall to fall, children offstage can tug the strings and all the boxes will collapse.

(Narrator enters and stands to one side of the stage, where he remains for the play.)

NARRATOR: Boys and girls, has anyone ever told you that God is strong and powerful and can do greater things than you can even think about? God is doing wonderful things for people all over the world, even while I'm talking to you, and the Bible is full of stories about the great things He has done in the past. All through history He has taken care of His people, and helped them when they were in trouble.

Once, a long time ago, when a man named Joshua was leader of God's people, God did an amazing thing to prove to them that He was powerful and they could trust Him to care for them.

The people of God were in a war with some other people who were living on their land. They had to take their land back from these people, but it seemed impossible because their enemies lived in a city named Jericho with a huge wall around it, much too big for Joshua's army to climb or break down. But here's what happened.

(Joshua enters on one side of the stage while the messenger enters, with his sword drawn, from the other side and stops a few steps from the entrance. Joshua is looking down and does not see him at first. When he is about to bump into him, he looks up and is startled by him.)

NARRATOR: Now when Joshua was near Jericho, he looked up and saw a man standing in front of him with a drawn sword in his hand. Joshua asked him . . .

JOSHUA: Are you on our side or the side of our enemies?

NARRATOR: The man answered . . .

MESSENGER: Neither, but as commander of the Lord's army I have now come.

(Joshua is overcome with awe and falls at his feet.)

NARRATOR: Now Joshua knew that this meant that the man was no ordinary person at all, but one of God's messengers. He asked him . . .

JOSHUA: What message does the Lord have for His servant?

MESSENGER: I have delivered Jericho into your hands, along with its king and all its fighting men.

(Joshua and Messenger exit, with Messenger talking and Joshua listening intently while Narrator continues.)

NARRATOR: This messenger of God explained exactly what Joshua must do to win the battle against Jericho.

(Israelite army enters and begins marching in front of the wall, disappearing offstage and reentering from the other side each time, as if they have walked around it. First comes the guard, then the seven priests with the horns, then the rest. This marching continues for the whole time Narrator speaks.)

NARRATOR: You might have thought the Lord would have just told Joshua to attack the city right away, but that's not what happened at all. Joshua got the strangest orders he'd ever heard. Here's what he had to do: He had to tell the whole army to march around the city once a day for six whole days. Then, on the seventh day, they had to march around the city seven times, and then the priests were to blow their horns and the people were to shout as loudly as they could. Then, after all that, they were to attack Jericho. But the most amazing part of what the messenger told Joshua was that the huge wall around Jericho was going to fall to the ground when they blew their horns!

Do you think you would believe anyone if they told you that the Lord was going to make a huge wall fall down? You can bet that some of God's people were wondering as they spent all those days marching around the wall, but they had already heard of many great things that the Lord had done, so they trusted Him and obeyed the orders.

Joshua did just as the messenger told him, and the army marched around the city for six days—the armed guards in front *(Guards wave to audience.)*, seven priests behind them *(Priests wave to audience.)*, and all the rest of the people of God behind them. *(All the people wave.)*

And on the seventh day, they marched around the city seven times.

(The army will march around seven more times, as fast as possible [run quietly backstage!] so it doesn't get boring. The front of the line can reenter without waiting for the back to clear offstage; just keep it orderly. Each time they march. Joshua will call out a line, and the army will repeat the number seven times, getting louder on each trip across the stage.)

JOSHUA: *One!* For all the miracles the Lord has done.

ALL: One, one, one, one, one, one, one.

JOSHUA: *Two!* For all the scrapes that He's pulled us through,

ALL: Two, two, two, two, two, two, two.

JOSHUA: *Three!* For all the victories we're gonna see,

ALL: Three, three, three, three, three, three, three.

JOSHUA: *Four!* For all the blessings that He has in store.

ALL: Four, four, four, four, four, four, four.

JOSHUA: *Five!* For crossing rivers and being kept alive,

ALL: Five, five, five, five, five, five, five.

JOSHUA: *Six!* For sending quails and making snakes from sticks,

ALL: Six, six, six, six, six, six, six.

JOSHUA: *Seven!* Because His people have a home in Heaven.

ALL *(shouting at the top of their lungs):* Seven!!!!!

(All stop, face the wall, and shout at top volume. Horns blast. Backstage people pull strings and the wall falls down. Israelites shout "Hooray," "The Lord did it," etc. and run off-stage. After the noise dies down, Narrator finishes.

NARRATOR: So the people of God captured the city of Jericho, and learned that God is great and powerful.

Questions for Discussion

1. Who was Joshua?

2. Who did he meet outside Jericho?

3. What did the Messenger of God tell Joshua to do?

4. Did Joshua do what the Messenger told him to do?

5. How long did they march around the wall?

6. What happened when the priests blew their horns and the people shouted?

7. What do you learn about God from this story?

I'm Nice to Everybody

This play is a conversation between two main characters, Tony and Anna, who have quite a few lines to memorize. It aims to teach children that what they *learn* about kindness must be *applied* before it becomes real. Also, a truly nice person is nice to family and familiar friends as well as to strangers. Adults may also find the play amusing.

Characters
TONY—a boy who is definitely not nice! (Many lines.)

ANNA—Tony's friend.

MOTHER

FREDDIE—Tony's little brother.

RICKY

Costumes
Ordinary clothing. Something has to identify the mother if the part is not played by an adult—an apron or something.

Props
A baseball and a mitt, or two coloring books and crayons, a few dollars.

The play can be performed with no set, or you could have a set near one entrance suggesting front porch and door; and along the back wall, a backdrop of a street scene with two stores at the other end of the stage, so when characters walk, there is the suggestion of distance covered.

(Tony and Anna are on Tony's front porch, talking and either tossing a baseball or coloring in coloring books. If there is no

porch, they can be standing and tossing the ball, or sitting in chairs to color.)

ANNA: How come you didn't come to Sunday school yesterday?

TONY: We went to see my Grandma. She lives far away so we had to leave early in the morning. What kind of cookies did you have?

ANNA: Chocolate with sprinkles. And we made these cards for our moms and Mrs. Fullton talked about being nice to everyone.

TONY: Well, I didn't need to go then, because I'm always nice to everyone.

ANNA *(thinks for a minute):* You're not always nice to me.

TONY: Well, you're always around. I don't always have to be nice to you.

ANNA: So you're nice to everyone but me?

TONY: Yeah.

(Tony's mother enters from the front door.)

MOTHER: Tony, I need some milk and eggs. Would you please go to the store for me?

TONY: Oh Mom, I don't want to go to the store—it's too hot.

MOTHER: Tony, I need them.

TONY *(in a nasty voice):* I don't care.

MOTHER *(angry):* Don't you speak to me like that! You take this money right now *(Hands him money.),* and you get to the store, and when you come back you will be spending the rest of the day inside because you were rude to me.

(She exits into the house. Tony looks surly.)

ANNA: You weren't very nice to her.

TONY: Well, she bugs me. She makes me do stuff I don't want to do.

(They begin walking slowly, as if walking to the store.)

ANNA: So you're nice to everyone but me and your mom?

TONY: Yeah.

(Freddie enters and runs after them.)

FREDDIE: Hey Tony! *(Tony ignores him.)* Hey Tony, Tony, wait for me. Hey Tony, can I come?

TONY: Get lost, Freddie.

FREDDIE: Aw, let me come Tony. I got nothing to do.

TONY *(louder):* I said, get lost! I'm sick of you always hanging around and getting in the way—go on!

(Freddie backs off and exits, looking hurt.)

ANNA: Well, Tony, you're not very nice to him either.

TONY: Well, he's just my little brother. He doesn't count.

ANNA: OK, so you're nice to everyone but me and your mom and your brother?

TONY: Yeah.

(Ricky enters from the opposite direction. As they pass, Tony jeers at him and makes a face.)

TONY: Hey Goober! *(Or whatever insulting term is popular.)* Where'd you get that Halloween mask on your face?

RICKY: Would you just leave me alone Tony? *(He exits.)*

ANNA: Tony, you can't tell me you were nice to him!

TONY: Yeah, but that's Ricky.

ANNA: So?

TONY: Well, you know Ricky. He's stupid.

ANNA: That's only what you think. You don't even know him! So you're not nice to people you think are stupid either. You're nice to everyone but me, your mom, your brother, and stupid people.

TONY: Yeah.

ANNA: Well, here we are at the store. *(She stops.)*

TONY: No, come on. We have to go to the next store.

ANNA: Why?

TONY: Because the last time I came to this store I stuck two loaves of bread together with my chewed up gum, and Mr. Weaver caught me and told me never to come back.

ANNA *(exasperated):* Well that wasn't a very nice thing to do either! Tony, just tell me one thing, who *are* you nice to?

TONY *(considers for a minute):* I'm nice to everybody in the whole world—just except for the people I know.

ANNA: Tony, if you're not nice to the people you know best, you can't be nice to anybody!

TONY: What do you mean?

ANNA: Well, it's easy to be nice to people you don't know very well; you don't have to live with them and see their faults. You're only really nice if you know people's faults and you can still love them.

TONY *(thinks, then nods with understanding):* Oh. Maybe I should have gone to that Sunday school class after all.

(Tony and Anna exit off stage.)

Questions for Discussion

1. What did Anna tell Tony she had learned in Sunday school last week?

2. How did Tony answer when she told him?

3. How did Tony treat his mother/little brother/Ricky/the man who ran the store?

4. How do you think he made each of them feel?

5. Do you think Tony was a nice person?

6. What did Anna mean when she told Tony that if you're not nice to the people you know best, then you're not nice at all?

7. What can you do if you are finding it hard to be nice to someone you know well?

Living Like Jesus

This play, which has only three children's parts and two parts for older people, stresses the importance of putting faith into practice. It shows children in three situations, behaving in ways that do not represent Jesus' behavior. You will probably need fifth or sixth graders to handle these parts; though there aren't many lines, the children must project themselves into imaginary situations and make their movements and expressions follow the narration.

Characters

NARRATOR—A teenager or adult, an animated storyteller.

TEACHER—A teenager or adult.

BILLY

TINA

CARMEN

Costumes

Ordinary clothing.

Props

A Bible and four chairs or boxes lined upstage center.

Narrator enters and stands center.

NARRATOR: Ladies and Gentlemen, Boys and Girls; since the time Jesus was living on the earth, we have known that the way to please God is not just to believe the right things, but to do the right things—to live as Jesus did. Now, even though we've had 2000 years for this lesson to sink in, some of us still have some trouble. Take this Sunday-school class, for example. . . .

(Teacher and four children enter in a line as Narrator steps to one side of the stage. All are holding their heads up high and looking proper. Children sit on chairs or boxes and focus on Teacher, who is holding an open Bible.)

NARRATOR: Now none of these children have any trouble believing in Jesus. . . .

TEACHER *(reading):* John 3:16 says, "For God loved the world so much that he gave his only Son, so that everyone who believes in him may not die but have eternal life." *(To children.)* Who really believes that Jesus is God's Son, and if we trust in Him we'll live forever?

(Children respond enthusiastically, throwing up their hands and saying, "Me, me," "I do, I do," etc.)

NARRATOR: As you can see, the children are enthusiastic about believing in Jesus.

TEACHER *(reading):* Good. Romans 3:23 and 24 says: "Everyone has sinned and is far away from God's saving presence. But by the free gift of God's grace all are put right with him through Christ Jesus, who sets them free." *(To children.)* Who really believes that we are cut off from God because of our sin, but God sent Jesus to die for us and save us?

(Children react with even more enthusiasm than before.)

NARRATOR: As you can see, the children were very enthusiastic about believing in Jesus.

TEACHER: Well I'm glad to hear that. *(Reading.)* John 14:6 says, "I am the way, the truth, and the life; no one goes to the Father except by me." *(To children.)* Who really believes that Jesus is the only way to God, and that everything He said was true?

(Children give their most enthusiastic reaction yet—much larger than life; waving arms, standing up, etc.)

81

NARRATOR: As you can see, the children were incredibly enthusiastic about believing in Jesus.

TEACHER: Well that's wonderful. I'm very glad to have a class full of children who believe in Jesus. Now I have one more passage I want you to hear, because it tells those who believe in Jesus how they must live. *(Reading.)* 1 John 2:4-6, "If someone says that he knows God, but does not obey his commands, such a person is a liar and there is no truth in him. . . . This is how we can be sure we are in union with God: whoever says that he remains in union with God should live just as Jesus Christ did." *(To children.)* So children, if you believe in Jesus, you have to live like He did. As you go home and begin this week, keep in mind all you know about Jesus, and pray that God will help you act the way Jesus would.

(Teacher closes Bible and exits. Children turn so their backs are to the audience.)

NARRATOR: Now all these children, who were so enthusiastic about believing in Jesus, went home after church that morning.

(Billy rises, brings his chair to center stage and sits, facing the audience.)

NARRATOR: Billy had the teacher's words about living like Jesus ringing in his ears—until he noticed that his little sister had some of her stuff on his half of the car seat.

(Billy looks down to one side, as though at a car seat he is sitting on, and frowns. Then he looks up, as if at his sister sitting next to him.)

BILLY: Get your junk off my side of the car.

NARRATOR: Billy figured that everyone knows that brothers and sisters have a line down the center of the back seat, and it is not a good idea to cross it. But Billy's sister did the unthinkable. Not only did she leave her stuff on his side of the car seat—she put her hand there too. Billy's reaction was swift.

(Billy mimes smacking his sister's hand and shoving her things over. Then he rises, paces to the other side of the stage, stops with his profile to the audience, crosses his arms, and frowns.)

NARRATOR: Now those of you who know anything about the way Jesus treated people would realize that Jesus would not have done that. So let's roll this scene back . . .

(Billy unfolds his arms, pulls his head up, paces backwards to his seat, sits, mimes the pushing motion backwards, then the slap, then freezes, looking sideways at his sister with a neutral expression.)

NARRATOR: . . . And see what would happen if Billy had stopped to think about living like Jesus.

(Narrator moves nearer Billy and speaks as his thoughts, in a softer voice.)

NARRATOR: First he might have thought of the time when Jesus said, "Love your neighbor as yourself."

BILLY: Oh yeah.

NARRATOR: And then, he probably would have decided that it really didn't matter whose side her stuff was on, and instead of hitting her, he might have said something like:

BILLY: Hey, that's a pretty neat book. Can you read that?

(Narrator smiles and moves back to the sidelines as Billy returns with his chair to its original position and sits with back to audience. At the same time, Tina brings her chair to the front, sits, and pretends to be watching a TV in front of her.)

NARRATOR: Tina had the teacher's words about living like Jesus ringing in her ears—until later that afternoon, when she was watching a Tarzan movie and her mom asked her to set the table for dinner . . .

TINA *(eyes glued to TV):* What Mom?

NARRATOR: . . . And Tarzan was about to save Jane from an elephant stampede. . . .

TINA *(speaking to the next room):* Right now?

NARRATOR: Tina figured everyone knows that you can't walk out of a Tarzan movie, even if it is three minutes till dinner, your mom is desperate for help, and you knew you had to set the table an hour ago. Tina's reaction was emotional.

TINA *(yelling):* You're just picking on me—you knew this was the best part of the movie! I'm not doing it!

(Tina rises, kicks her chair, stomps over to the other side of the stage, stops where Billy did, and adopts the same stance.)

NARRATOR: Now those of you who know anything about how gentle Jesus was would realize that Jesus would not have done that. So let's roll back this scene . . .

(Tina unfolds her arms, puts her head up, stomps backwards to her chair, kicks it, sits and mimes watching TV with a neutral expression.)

NARRATOR: . . . And see what would have happened if Tina had stopped to think about living like Jesus.

(Narrator moves nearer to Tina and speaks as her thoughts, in a softer voice.)

NARRATOR: First she might have thought about the time when Jesus said, "If anyone wants to follow Me, he must deny himself."

TINA: Oh yeah.

NARRATOR: Then she might have thought about how Jesus would spend hour after hour serving people; teaching them and healing them and talking with them, without even having a home to go back to for rest.

TINA *(ashamed):* Oh yeah.

NARRATOR: And then, she probably would have decided that it really didn't matter if she missed a few minutes of a Tarzan movie, and instead of yelling at her mother, she may have said something like . . .

TINA: OK Mom. Do I use place mats or a tablecloth?

(Narrator smiles and moves back to the sidelines. Tina returns with her chair to its original position and sits with her back to the audience. At the same time, Carmen brings her chair up to the front and sits in it, miming drawing a picture at a desk.)

NARRATOR: Now Carmen had the teacher's words about living like Jesus ringing in her ears—until the next day in school, when she and her friend were drawing pictures in class, and Carmen noticed that her picture was better than her friend's.

CARMEN *(pointing down at her friend's picture):* What's that supposed to be?

NARRATOR: And Carmen's friend told her it was a camel, as anyone can see.

CARMEN: Well, my camel looks more real.

NARRATOR: Carmen figured that everyone knows what a camel is supposed to look like, and that since hers was better, her friend should just admit it. Carmen's reaction was confident.

CARMEN: Your picture doesn't look anything like a camel. It looks like a cow with a lumpy back. My pictures are always better than yours. So there.

(Carmen tosses her head, gets up, and flounces over to the other side of the stage with her nose in the air. She stops where the others did and adopts the same stance.)

NARRATOR: Now those of you who know anything about how kind Jesus was would realize that Jesus would not have done that. So let's roll this scene back . . .

(Carmen unfolds her arms, pulls her chin in, flounces backwards to her seat, sits down, tosses her head, and looks at her friend with a neutral expression.)

NARRATOR: . . . And see what would have happened if she had stopped to think about living like Jesus.

(Narrator moves nearer to Carmen and speaks as her thoughts, in a softer voice.)

NARRATOR: First she might have thought about the time when Jesus said, "Everyone who makes himself great will be humbled."

CARMEN: Oh yeah.

NARRATOR: Then she might have thought about how when Jesus was in Jerusalem and the leaders of the Jews were lying about Him and plotting to kill Him—He never bothered to defend himself, even though He was the Son of God.

CARMEN *(ashamed):* Oh yeah.

NARRATOR: And then, Carmen probably would have decided that it really didn't matter whose camel was better, and instead of saying mean things to her friend, probably would have said something like . . .

CARMEN: That's a good idea—having a man riding the camel.

(Narrator smiles and returns to the sidelines as Carmen returns with her chair to its original position. Then all three children come to the front and face the audience together.)

NARRATOR: So Ladies and Gentlemen, Boys and Girls, it isn't enough just to believe in Jesus, because . . .

ALL CHILDREN: . . . whoever says that he remains in union with God should live just as Jesus Christ did.

Questions for Discussion

1. Did all the children in the class believe in Jesus?

2. What was the last thing the teacher told them before they went home?

3. What did Billy do wrong?

4. What would he have done if he had thought about living like Jesus?

5. What did Tina do wrong?

6. What would she have done instead if she had thought about living like Jesus?

7. What did Carmen do wrong?

8. What would she have done instead if she had thought about living like Jesus?

9. Read 1 John 2:4-6. What do these verses say about people who believe in God but don't obey Him?

The Parable of the Weeds

This is a dramatization of the parable of the weeds found in Matthew 13. A narrator tells the parable while children act as characters, wheat and seeds, taking their cues from the narration. By acting out and explaining the parable, children should understand that parables have messages that are relevant to them.

Characters

NARRATOR—a teenager or adult who is a good storyteller.

FARMER

ENEMY

WHEAT—Four children who can somersault and are good at mime.

WEEDS—Four more of the above.

SERVANTS—Two children.

Costumes

The farmer should wear a flannel shirt, overalls, and a hat. The enemy can wear a black hat, a mask, and a cape. Wheat and weeds don't really need costumes, but they could wear the same colors: light brown and beige for wheat, green or dark brown for weeds. Their clothing needs to allow freedom of movement.

Props

None.

Narrator enters and addresses the audience.

NARRATOR: Today we are going to learn about the Kingdom of Heaven. Who knows what the Kingdom of Heaven is? Has anyone ever visited there? No, because when the Bible talks about the Kingdom of Heaven, it isn't exactly talking about a place. We don't have to go anywhere to enter the Kingdom of Heaven. We can enter it by deciding to accept Jesus as our Savior, and by being obedient to His commands. When we live our lives to please the Lord instead of ourselves, we have entered the Kingdom of Heaven.

Now Jesus taught us about the Kingdom of Heaven using little stories, called parables. For example: once He said, "The Kingdom of Heaven is like this," and then He told a story about a farmer in his field.

(Farmer enters and looks around, smiling with satisfaction.)

NARRATOR: Now this farmer had a bunch of seeds.

(Wheat seeds somersault or roll on stage from left and stop, clustered together, in "round" positions, with legs curled up, arms wrapped around them, and heads tucked in. Farmer smiles proudly at them.)

NARRATOR: The farmer was very proud of his wheat. He had saved his seeds from last year's best crop, so they were very good seeds. One by one he planted them in his field.

(Farmer takes seeds one by one and rolls them into a line across the stage's central area, about two yards apart. The "seeds" should land on their feet. Once in place, seeds lift their heads to show beaming smiles, which they retain throughout the play.)

NARRATOR: But one night, after those good seeds had been planted, an enemy, who was evil, snuck into the farmer's field while he was asleep.

(As Narrator speaks, Farmer lays on the floor and falls asleep to one extreme side of the stage, while Enemy tiptoes into the field, looking furtively around. He points to the good seeds, laughs nastily and rubs his hands together.)

NARRATOR: Then the enemy did a terrible thing. He brought in some weed seeds . . .

(Enemy beckons offstage and weed seeds somersault on and cluster together in the same way as the wheat seeds did.)

NARRATOR: . . . and he took those bad seeds, and he planted them right along with the farmer's beautiful wheat seeds— all mixed in together!

(As he speaks, Enemy takes the weed seeds one by one and rolls them in place between the wheat seeds. Once in place, the weed seeds lift their heads to reveal ugly, contorted expressions, which they will retain throughout the play. Enemy surveys his work, laughs gleefully, and exits.)

NARRATOR: Now you know what happened next. The seeds began to grow—both the good seeds and the weeds, and the bigger they got, the more clearly you could see which were wheat and which were weeds.

(As Narrator speaks, the seeds all begin growing slowly, rising and stretching out their arms. The wheat finish standing straight, with their arms up straight towards the sky, still smiling. The weeds finish in crooked positions, retaining their ugly faces. As this is happening, Farmer rises and watches with a disturbed expression.)

NARRATOR: The farmer was very upset to see the ugly weeds growing in his beautiful field. His servants came to him . . .

(Servants enter and approach the farmer.)

NARRATOR: . . . and said, "Sir, you planted good seeds in your field. Where did these weeds come from?"

SERVANT #1: Sir, I thought you planted only good seeds in your field.

SERVANT #2: Yeah, where did these ugly, old weeds come from?

NARRATOR: The farmer knew that some enemy must have done this.

FARMER: Some enemy must have done this.

NARRATOR: He knew that if he pulled the weeds, some of the wheat might get pulled up too, before it had a chance to grow. So he decided to let the weeds and wheat grow together until it was harvest time.

FARMER: Let them grow together until the harvest.

NARRATOR: And do you know what happened in the fall, at harvest, when it was time to cut the wheat? The farmer had the wheat gathered up . . .

(Servants enter with a rope, take each piece of wheat by the shoulders, and the wheat inches along with little sideways steps, still smiling, to where they are guided. The servants gather them into a cluster near the exit and tie a rope around them.)

NARRATOR: . . . and put it into the barn . . .

(Servants tug the wheat off left and Farmer exits with them.)

NARRATOR: . . . and then he had the weeds gathered up . . .

(Servants reenter, gather and tie the weeds up in the same way as they did with the wheat.)

NARRATOR: . . . and carried away.

(Servants tug the weeds off right.)

NARRATOR: Now that is the end of the story, except that Jesus also explained what the parable meant.

FARMER *(reentering):* He said the farmer in the story was like God, and the farmer's field was the world.

ONE WHEAT SEED *(as all seeds reenter):* The good seeds are like the people who love God and live for Him.

ONE WEED *(as all weeds reenter):* The weeds are like people who do not live for God but do evil.

ENEMY *(reentering):* The enemy is Satan.

SERVANT #1 *(as both reenter):* The servants are like God's angels.

NARRATOR: And the end of the story, when the wheat and weeds are gathered, is like the end of the age, when those who have not lived for God are taken away where they cannot be with Him, and the people who belong to God are taken to live with Him forever.

So, whenever you hear a story that Jesus told, you will know that it has a meaning that will teach you something about the Kingdom of Heaven. So when you hear a parable, think about it carefully and learn what the Lord has to teach you from it.

Questions for Discussion

1. What is a parable?

2. Who planted the good seeds?

3. Who planted the weed seeds?

4. What did the farmer do when he found out that the weeds were mixed in with his wheat?

5. Who is the farmer in the story like?

6. Who are the good seeds like?

7. Who is the enemy like?

8. Who are the weed seeds like?

9. What does this parable say will happen to people who love God and do good, and to people who ignore God and do evil? (Point out that good and evil are not a matter of works but acceptance or rejection of Christ.)

Praying

This is a simple, short skit consisting of five children talking about prayer. All the children have several lines to memorize. Because it is so important for children to realize they can have a personal relationship with God, the play aims to teach them that they can bring all aspects of their lives before God when they pray. It contrasts this attitude with the limitations of rote prayer.

The ending of the play is left open so that the children can have a spontaneous prayer time. This is because a scripted prayer would become a rote prayer. Discuss with them the sort of concerns and burdens and praise they can bring to God, and make sure they are used to praying as a group before they pray before an audience.

Characters
Five children, all of whom must be expressive and able to remember lines.

Costumes
Ordinary clothing.

Props
None.

John enters and walks to center stage, closes eyes, folds hands, and prays aloud.

JOHN *(without much feeling):* Now I lay me down to sleep, I pray the Lord my soul to keep. If I should die before I wake, I pray the Lord my soul to take. Amen.

(As John prays, Carol enters and listens.)

CAROL *(when he's finished):* Do you always say that prayer?

John: Yeah. Every night. Don't you?

Carol: No, but I say one at dinner. I say *(assuming praying position)* "God is great, God is good, and we thank Him for our food. Amen."

(As Carol is praying, Leah enters and listens.)

John *(to Leah):* Do you have a prayer that you say?

Leah: Yes, I always say *(assumes praying position)*, "Dear God, thank You for a nice day. Bless Daddy and Mommy and Rachael and Jeff and Grandma and Grandpa and my cat. Amen."

(As Leah prays, Pam and Daryl enter and listen. Make sure they are naturally grouped, not in a straight line.)

Leah *(to Pam and Daryl):* What prayers do you say?

Pam: I can't remember the prayer I'm supposed to say. Grandma tells me but I forget.

Carol *(to Daryl):* Do you have a prayer?

Daryl: No.

(All show surprise, ad-lib "No prayer?" etc.)

Carol: Don't you ever pray?

Daryl: Sure, I pray all the time, but I don't say just one prayer. I pray about everything.

Pam: Are you supposed to do that?

Daryl: Sure you are. My dad told me the Bible says you're supposed to pray about everything. He said God loves us and He wants us to talk to Him all the time.

John: Really? What do you say to Him?

Daryl: Well, you thank Him for things, you ask Him to forgive you when you do wrong, and you pray for other people. You tell Him about your problems too, and just whatever's on your mind. Just like a friend, except He's much greater than a person.

(Children react with pleasure and interest.)

CAROL: Wow, do you mean He really listens, all the time?

DARYL: Yeah.

LEAH: And does He really forgive you, and really help you when you ask Him to?

DARYL: Yes, the Bible says that too.

PAM: Well that's really neat. I'm going to talk to God a lot now.

LEAH: So am I.

CAROL: Me too.

JOHN: Let's talk to Him now.

(The children pray.)

Questions for Discussion

1. Did all the children have just one prayer that they said to the Lord?

2. What was the reason Daryl didn't have just one prayer?

3. What did Daryl say that the Bible tells us about praying?

4. What kinds of things can we thank God for?

5. What kinds of things do we need to ask God to forgive us for?

6. What can we ask God for when we pray for others?

7. What kinds of problems can you talk to God about?

8. When you pray, do you think God will answer in a voice you can hear with your ears? (Clarify that God is still present even though we can't hear or see Him.)

Hilda
the Good-for-Nothing Bunny

This is a play which illustrates that differences in looks and abilities are positive and part of what makes everyone special. Hilda, a bunny is ostracized by a group of mean mice until a crisis teaches them that bunnies aren't good-for-nothing after all. The play also shows how damaging put-downs are.

Characters

NARRATOR—A good storyteller, has most of the lines.

HILDA—The main character, needs to be expressive.

NICE MOUSE—A part with six lines.

BIG CHEESE—A part with one monologue.

MICE—A group of anywhere between six and twenty children. Their lines are numbered from one to twenty in the script, and you can designate them any way you like.

Costumes

The narrator can wear casual or dressy clothes depending on the event at which the play is presented. Costumes for one bunny and all mice will be needed. They can be as elaborate as your resources allow, or as simple as ears and tails. For instance, you can cut ears out of colored cardboard and staple them to elastic headbands. Mouse tails can be made from paper-stuffed panty hose legs. Mouse whiskers can be drawn on with eyeliner. Hilda will need big ears and a puffy tail.

Props

A giant carrot, preferably larger-than-life.
Two blocks will be needed for set pieces, placed lengthwise, center stage. If necessary, the narrator can "cheat" by reading the script if you hide it with a fairy-tale-like book cover.

Narrator enters and stands to one side of the stage.

NARRATOR: Once upon a time there was a mouse village, hidden under a tall tree at the bottom of a shady garden.

(Mice enter in groups of three or four, talking to each other. They arrange themselves in three separate groups, USR, UC, and USL.)

NARRATOR: The mice all got along with each other pretty well. Now, there also lived, in the same shady garden, a bunny named Hilda.

(Hilda hops on L and pauses SL, looking at the mice.)

NARRATOR: Hilda was a very nice bunny, but she was lonely. There were no other bunnies in that garden. She wanted to be friends with the mice, but they picked on her because she was different.

(As Narrator speaks, Hilda hops DC. The mice converge on her and insult her.)

MOUSE 1 *(poking Hilda)*: Well, look who's here. It's Hilda, the good-for-nothing-bunny.

MOUSE 2 *(pulling her ears):* What happened to your ears—did your mom buy them five sizes too big?

(Other mice giggle.)

MOUSE 3 *(spinning her around so her back is showing):* Hey Hilda, you call that thing a tail? It looks like someone dunked your rear end in cotton candy!

(Other mice laugh. Hilda looks hurt, as all the mice chant.)

MICE: Hilda's just a bunny, she looks really funny!

(Mice laugh as Hilda, upset, runs away to DSL. They begin to exit R, looking over their shoulders and talking about Hilda as they go.)

MOUSE 4: She is so weird.

MOUSE 5: You know, I heard they don't even eat cheese.

MOUSE 6: You're kidding!

(After they exit, Hilda walks sadly back to C.)

NARRATOR: It was always like that. The mice would either pick on Hilda, or ignore her completely. They never let her in on anything they were doing. It wasn't that Hilda didn't try to make friends. She really did. Once, when she was out looking for something to eat, she found the biggest carrot she had ever seen!

(As Narrator is talking, Hilda looks around the ground on stage, and brings out a huge carrot from behind the block. She looks at it with admiration.)

NARRATOR: Hilda got an idea.

HILDA: I know! I'll give this terrific carrot to the mice. Then maybe they'll know that I want to be friends and I'm not good-for-nothing.

(She moves USC and begins to look offstage.)

NARRATOR: She waited a long time for some mice to show up. Finally two mice came walking along the path. Hilda got up her courage and talked to them.

(The mice enter R and pass in front of Hilda, ignoring her, she calls them and they stop, turn and look at her in surprise.)

HILDA: Uh, excuse me, little mice!

MOUSE 7: What do you want, Big Bunny?

HILDA: Uh, I found this terrific carrot, and I, I wanted to give it to all the mice for a present.

(Mice look at each other and roll their eyes.)

MOUSE 8: Mice don't eat carrots.

HILDA (disappointed): Oh. I didn't think of that.

MOUSE 9: Dumb bunny.

(The mice continue on their way and exit L. Hilda looks dejected.)

NARRATOR: Whenever the mice treated her like that, Hilda felt really hurt. She would stay away from them for a long time, but then she would get so lonely that she'd decide to try again.

One day, Hilda was feeling really lonely, and she decided to sneak down to the mouse village, just to see what was going on.

(Hilda exits R.)

As she got nearer, she heard the sound of terrific music coming from the Mouse Lodge. Hilda was so lonely, and the music sounded so good, she dared to peek into the lodge to see what was going on. There she saw a band playing square dance music, and a bunch of mice dancing around wildly.

(As Narrator says the last sentence, mice enter, dancing in square dance formations (ie. clapping, stomping, hooking arms together and skipping in circles). They are having a lot of fun. Three of them jump up on the blocks and mime playing a banjo, bass and fiddle. Hilda sticks her head and shoulders onstage, R.)

NARRATOR: Well, when Hilda saw all that, and how much fun they were having, she forgot that the mice didn't like her, and she ran in and started dancing too! The trouble was, Hilda was a whole lot bigger than the mice, and without meaning to, she bumped into them, and stepped on their tails, and even knocked a few over.

(As Narrator speaks, Hilda does what is described. Mice are shocked, then angry. They stop dancing and back into a semi-circle around Hilda.)

MOUSE 10: What's that rabbit doing in here?

MOUSE 11: She stepped on my tail!

MOUSE 12: She messed up my whiskers!

MOUSE 13: She knocked me down!

MOUSE 14: Get rid of her before she puts us in the hospital!

(They all yell "Get out", etc., and drive Hilda off SR. Then they all exit SL, talking as they go.)

MOUSE 15: What a nerve, crashing our party.

MOUSE 16: She's totally good-for-nothing.

NARRATOR: Hilda hopped out of the lodge. She felt so crushed and miserable that tears filled up her eyes and she couldn't see where she was going. She stumbled into the forest and buried her face in her furry paws. She started crying and once she started, she couldn't stop.

(Hilda reenters on Narrator's mention of the forest, sits on a block and cries.)

HILDA: I'm so sad and lonely! I wish someone, somewhere, would like me the way I am!

NARRATOR: Now, it so happened that one of the mice was taking a walk through the forest, and he saw Hilda sitting there crying. He stopped and looked at her curiously.

(As Narrator speaks, Nice Mouse enters L, sees Hilda and pauses to her left.)

NICE MOUSE: Something wrong with you, Bunny?

HILDA *(looking up, surprised):* Yeeeees.

NICE MOUSE: Are you crying?

HILDA: Yeeees.

NICE MOUSE: I didn't know bunnies cried too. Why are you crying?

HILDA: Because no one will be my friend. Everyone picks on me because I'm different.

NICE MOUSE *(sitting next to her):* You mean bunnies can feel lonely and sad like mice?

HILDA: Of course! Boy, I wish something would happen to show mice that bunnies aren't good-for-nothing!

NICE MOUSE: Maybe we shouldn't have been so mean. You seem pretty nice. Hilda, I'm sorry.

HILDA *(surprised):* You are?

NICE MOUSE: Yeah, I really am. I'm gonna go tell the other mice we've been jerks to pick on you.

(Nice Mouse exits R. Hilda watches after him, smiling.)

NARRATOR: Well it was a wonderful thing to have someone being nice to her. Hilda cheered up right away. But she didn't have long to think about it, because suddenly she heard a sound coming from down in the village.

(From offstage R, loud squeaking is heard. Hilda exits R.)

Down in the village, a terrible thing was happening. Two terrifying creatures called a Boy and a Girl found the mice, chased them, and trapped them in a box!

(Mice enter R, running all over the stage, squealing in fear and looking up. They converge C, in front of the blocks, where they cower together. Then they begin talking and doing mime which defines the sides of a box.)

MOUSE 17: Hey, we're trapped!

MOUSE 18: There's no way out!

MOUSE 19: Oh no!

ALL MICE: Help! Somebody help us!

(Hilda reenters R.)

NARRATOR: This is how Hilda found the mice when she got to the village.

HILDA: Oh, no, the mice are trapped in a big box! They're too little to climb out!

(She runs to the box.)

HILDA: Quick, little mice, before they come back! Hop! You'll have to hop out!

MICE: We can't hop!

MOUSE 20: Dumb Bunny.

HILDA: Oh yeah. *(Thinks for a minute, then brightens up.)* But I can hop!

NARRATOR: And that's exactly what Hilda did. She hopped to the box, took a huge leap and crouched inside so the mice could run up her soft, furry back, stand on her head and get out over the top!

(As Narrator speaks, Hilda hops behind the mice, onto the block, which the mice must conceal, and crouches on the block. The mice stay crowded around her to conceal the block. Mice actually stand on a block and jump off the back of it. As they get out they come around the front of the box and stand with their backs to the audience, hands up against the "box," supposedly watching what is happening, so they can still conceal the blocks. Each time a mouse gets out, he shouts "I'm free!" and the Narrator says, "One mouse is out," "Two Mice are out," etc. until "All the mice are out!" Finally Hilda hops off the blocks and they all leap around joyfully, shouting "We made it!" "Hooray!", etc.)

HILDA: Quick, let's get out of here before they come back! I'll show you a safe hole!

(All the mice follow Hilda off L.)

NARRATOR: Hilda led the mice to a safe place, and when

104

everyone had gotten their breath back, the leader of the mice, Big Cheese, got up to make a speech.

(As Narrator speaks, all reenter L, mice following Hilda, and sit around the stage in a horseshoe shape around the blocks. Big Cheese stands on a block.)

BIG CHEESE: Fellow mice, something needs to be said. We have all made a terrible mistake. We have Hilda the bunny to thank for saving our lives, and we were wrong to pick on her for being different. If she hadn't been a bunny who could hop, we'd still be stuck in that box! Three cheers for Hilda!

MICE: Hip, hip, hurray! *(Three times.)*

(Hilda is led forward to shake hands with Big Cheese, then mice surround her, lift her up and carry her off R, still cheering. Narrator continues after they exit.)

NARRATOR: So the mice finally made friends with Hilda, and told her how sorry they were for being mean. She forgave them, and was very glad not to be lonely anymore. The mice made her the guest of honor at their next dance, and they all lived happily ever after.

Questions for Discussion

1. Why were the mice mean to Hilda?

2. How did Hilda feel when the mice picked on her?

3. Why did the mice change their minds about Hilda?

4. Are children ever mean to each other?

5. How do you feel when someone says something mean to you?

6. What are some things children say to each other to let each other know that they are special?

Jesus Is Here

All the characters in this play can be children. It is a simple play, but the actors have to be able to learn quite a few lines, especially Nancy.

This play's aim is to reinforce to the children that the Lord is always with them and that His presence should give them joy and affect their behavior.

Characters

NANCY—The main character. (Many lines.)

MOTHER—A child can play this part.

JENNY—A sad girl.

MICHAEL

DANNY

NEW GIRL—A shy girl. (Only one line.)

Costumes

Ordinary clothing. Mother can wear an apron or dress to look older.

Props

Two chairs.

The play begins with Nancy and Mother seated on chairs, halfway facing the audience and halfway facing one another. Nancy is looking at a Bible while her mother sews or something.

NANCY: Hey Mommy, what does it say under this picture of Jesus in the Bible?

MOTHER *(leans over and reads):* "I will be with you always, to the very end of the age."

NANCY: Who was He talking to?

MOTHER: He was talking to His followers at the time, but He means it for all people—everyone in the whole world.

NANCY: You mean He's here with us right now?

MOTHER: Yes, He is, wherever you are and whatever you're doing.

NANCY: But I've never seen Him.

MOTHER: Well, we can't see Him until we get to Heaven, but even though we can't see Him, we can be sure He is with us.

NANCY: Wow! That's great; I'm going to tell my friends that. Bye, Mom.

MOTHER: Bye, Nancy. Be careful if you cross the street!

(Mother exits with two chairs. Nancy circles the stage as if walking to another location. Then Jenny enters, walking with her head bowed and looking sad.)

NANCY *(approaching her):* What's the matter, Jenny? You look very sad. *(Puts her hand on Jenny's shoulder.)*

JENNY: I'm lonely. Everyone at home is too busy to talk.

NANCY: You shouldn't feel sad, Jenny, because you know what? Jesus is always here with you and you can always pray to Him!

JENNY: You mean He's here all the time and not just in church?

NANCY: Yeah, it says so in the Bible.

JENNY: Well I didn't know that! If Jesus is always with me, I'm never *really* alone, am I?

NANCY *(happily):* Nope!

JENNY: Well, I am really glad to know that!

(Two boys enter, shoving each other, arguing. They stop near Nancy and Jenny, who look surprised.)

DANNY: I hate your guts, Michael.

MICHAEL: I hate your guts, Danny.

DANNY: I'm gonna punch you right in the face!

(Danny prepares to punch; Jenny interrupts.)

JENNY: Hey, you guys, you shouldn't be fighting and saying such mean things to each other.

DANNY: I don't see why not—he's a jerk!

JENNY: But Jesus is here with us right now, and the way you're acting makes Him sad and angry. Did you know that?

MICHAEL: Jesus is here right now?

JENNY: Yeah, He's always with us.

DANNY: I didn't know that. I thought He was far away in Heaven.

JENNY: Well, He's here too—so get along with each other!

(The two boys look at each other apologetically.)

DANNY: OK, Michael, you can play with my racetrack if you want to. *(Or name a toy that is popular with your children.)*

(New Girl enters, and stands near stage entrance, looking shy.)

NANCY: Hey, that's the girl who just moved in down the street.

MICHAEL: Oh no, not another girl! I don't want to play with her.

JENNY: Michael. . . . *(They all look at him, smiling.)*

ALL: Jesus is here!

MICHAEL *(looking a little sheepish):* Oh yeah.

JENNY: Let's go play with her.

109

(They all move toward the new girl.)

MICHAEL: Hi, you want to play with us?

NEW GIRL: Sure! *(She looks happier.)*

NANCY: OK, let's go!

(They all exit, talking happily together.)

Questions for Discussion

1. What did Nancy's mother tell her Jesus said in the Bible?

2. Is Jesus with us only when we go to church and learn about Him?

3. Can we see Jesus? Does that mean He is not here?

4. What did Nancy do when she found out that Jesus is always with us?

5. How was Jenny feeling when Nancy first saw her?

6. How did Jenny feel when Nancy told her that Jesus was with her?

7. What did Danny and Michael do when they found out about Jesus always being with them? Why?

8. What did Michael do when he saw the new girl? Is this how Jesus wants us to act?